Sweet
and SAVORY

award-winning

RECIPES

made easy

- 1ST PLACE
Dream Dinners Contest

- 2ND PLACE
BBQ Lover's Contest

- 3RD PLACE
Utah's Own Ultimate
Recipe Roundup

Sweet

and SAVORY

Shauna Evans

Front Table Books | Springville, Utah

ISBN: 978-1-4621-1114-5

Published by Front Table Books, an imprint of Cedar Fort, Inc., 2373 W. 700 S., Springville, UT 84663
Distributed by Cedar Fort, Inc., www.cedarfort.com

LIBRARY OF CONGRESS CATALOGING-IN-PUBLICATION DATA ON FILE

Cover and page design by Erica Dixon
Cover design © 2013 by Lyle Mortimer
Edited and typeset by Casey J. Winters

Printed in China

10 9 8 7 6 5 4 3 2 1

To my mother and grandmothers, *wonderful* home cooks.

Contents

Introduction 1

Appetizers and Beverages 3

Soups, Salads, and Dressings 23

Side Dishes 49

Main Dishes 75

Breads and Rolls 133

Desserts 151

Breakfasts and Brunches 183

Index 199

About the Author 203

Introduction

Sweet and Savory is a compilation of recipes from three generations of home cooks. This cookbook is the result of a labor of love in the heart of the home. It all started with my two grandmothers, both of whom were excellent cooks and tremendous homemakers.

My maternal grandmother created bean with bacon tacos that are a family favorite. She always had a German chocolate cake on the counter. She enjoyed making lovely desserts for afternoon refreshment and chatting with her best friend and next-door neighbor, Loa Booth.

My paternal grandmother was a whiz in the kitchen. She made tasty homemade chocolate chip cookies for my grandfather and her grandsons each time they went fishing. There seemed to be a set Jell-O salad in the ice box each time we visited. However, it was her plum streusel and German potato salad that were legendary.

My mother continued in the tradition of preparing wonderful home-cooked food. Spaghetti, pizza, and chocolate pie all go to her credit. From the time I was five, I was making food in our kitchen. My first attempt at baking was a disaster. As a surprise to my family, I tried to make a pie. What I made was something that tasted like glue and hardened like cement. Thirty-five years later, my peach pie won third place for Utah's Own Ultimate Recipe Roundup at the state fair.

Even though my first effort was awful, I did not let that deter me, because I love food and creating delicious recipes for my family and friends. When I was in junior high, I was known for my gourmet sandwiches, like the Caesar salad sandwich. In high school, I learned to make simple meals and desserts—usually brownies—for my family. In college, I stepped it up and tried more complicated and challenging recipes, including our famous family fudge that won Utah Valley Magazine's Christmas Dessert Contest in December 2011.

Making delicious home-cooked food is easy if you have the right recipe. That is where *Sweet and Savory* comes into the mix. The purpose of this book: simple and scrumptious food that is quick and easy to prepare for busy moms and families. Recipes don't need to be complicated to be yummy. In fact, simple recipes are often the best. These recipes call for basic, pure ingredients that are readily available in local supermarkets. Many of the meals can be prepared in thirty minutes or less. I've also included tips to help with ease in preparation, and the photos will inspire and guide in creating the final product.

Home-cooked food is at your fingertips. We become connected as families and friends as we gather to share meals and memories. We are not only nourishing bodies but also nurturing relationships.

Enjoy these **sweet** and **savory** dishes!

Appetizers *and* **Beverages**

Artichoke Dip

This warm, savory appetizer is lovely for any occasion. Serve with pita chips. For a little chic presentation, warm and serve the dip in small cast-iron skillets. 16 servings.

1 (15-oz.) can non-marinated artichoke hearts
1 cup mayonnaise
1 cup fresh Parmesan cheese, grated
1 cup Monterey Jack cheese, shredded
1 (6-oz.) can green chilies, chopped
dash of garlic powder

1. **In microwave-safe bowl,** combine all ingredients.

2. **Refrigerate** dip until ready to use.

3. **Just before serving,** microwave dip until cheese is melted.

4

Shauna Evans

Bruschetta

Bruschetta is one of those Italian appetizers that Americans love. This is especially good with homegrown tomatoes and garden basil in season. 12 servings.

¼ cup butter
1 French baguette, cut into 1-inch slices
2 cups chopped fresh tomatoes
1 cup chopped fresh basil
¼ cup finely chopped fresh parsley
¼ cup extra-virgin olive oil
¼ tsp. cracked pepper
¼ cup grated Parmesan cheese

1. **In skillet,** melt butter on medium heat.

2. **Toast** each bread slice in butter over medium heat until golden brown.

3. **In bowl,** combine tomatoes, basil, parsley, oil, and pepper.

4. **Top** each bread slice with 1–2 tablespoons tomato mixture and a pinch of Parmesan.

5. **Place** tomato-topped bread slices on cookie sheet and broil in 375-degree oven for 1 minute or until cheese is melted.

Christmas Cheese Ball

My aunt would make this for our family Christmas party every year. She served it with butter crackers. This cheese ball is a classic. 16 servings.

2 (8-oz.) pkgs. cream cheese, softened
1 (8-oz.) pkg. sharp cheddar cheese, grated
⅛ cup pimentos, finely chopped
1 Tbsp. lemon juice
1 tsp. Worcestershire sauce
½ tsp. salt
1 tsp. fresh onion, grated
dash of cayenne pepper
¾ cup raw slivered almonds

1. **Mix** all ingredients except almonds.

2. **Shape** into ball.

3. **Roll** ball in almonds spread on a plate.

4. **Wrap** with plastic and chill for at least 3 hours.

6

Confetti Squares

This is a fun party finger food. It's colorful with a crisp and creamy texture. 24 servings.

2 (11.25-oz.) pkgs. refrigerated crescent rolls
2 (8-oz) pkgs. cream cheese, softened
⅔ cup mayonnaise
3 carrots, peeled and shredded
2 celery ribs, diced
½ sweet red pepper, diced
6 green onions, finely chopped
3 broccoli florets, chopped

1. **Pat** crescent dough onto a jelly roll pan and bake according to package directions.

2. **Let** dough cool completely.

3. **Beat** cream cheese and mayonnaise.

4. **Spread** cream cheese mixture evenly over baked roll dough.

5. **Sprinkle** veggies evenly on top of cream cheese mixture.

6. **Cut** into small pieces.

7. **Place** in refrigerator, covered, and chill for 3 hours before serving.

Grandma's Dill Dip

❧ Wise grandmothers have a way of sneaking vegetables into dishes for kids. Dill Dip was one way my grandmother got her grandchildren to gobble up an assortment of raw vegetables. It was this or Jell-O. And two generations later, my children will devour a plate of crudités (fresh-cut vegetables) in a snap if Dill Dip is served. 8 servings.

1 cup sour cream
1 cup mayonnaise
2 tsp. dried parsley leaves
2 tsp. dried onion, minced
2 tsp. dill weed
2 tsp. Bon Appetit seasoning salt

1. **Combine** all ingredients in a bowl.

2. **Chill**.

Shauna Evans

Old-Fashioned Lemonade

Who doesn't love old-fashioned lemonade? Lemonade is one of those things that you need to experience fresh and homemade. The frozen concentrates and powders are fine and serve their purpose, but the homemade variety should be enjoyed every summer by every child. Serve cold with lemon slices. 8 servings.

1 cup sugar
6 cups water (divided use)
juice of 4 lemons

1. **In small saucepan,** bring sugar and 2 cups water to a boil.

2. **Heat** until sugar is dissolved.

3. **Let** syrup cool in refrigerator for about 1 hour.

4. **Add** 4 cups ice-cold water and lemon juice to syrup and mix.

5. **Serve** cold with lemon slices.

Hummus

I fell deeply in love with hummus in London when my daughter and I happened upon "Hummus Brothers" for dinner. They make all things chickpeas, served with plates of soft pita bread for dipping. Their plea: "Give peas a chance." Hummus and pita bread is not just a Mediterranean staple, it's also a fabulous and healthy appetizer making way in the United States. Serve with pita bread, pita chips, or crudités. 8 servings.

    1 (16-oz.) can garbanzo beans (chickpeas)
    ¼ cup garbanzo bean liquid (reserved from can above)
    2 Tbsp. fresh lemon juice
    1½ Tbsp. soy sauce
    ½ tsp. salt
    2 Tbsp. extra virgin olive oil
    ¼ tsp. paprika

1. **Place** all ingredients except paprika in blender and pulse until smooth.
2. **Garnish** with a sprinkling of paprika.

French Herb Cheese and Ham Spirals

🍃 *French Herb Cheese and Ham Spirals are chic petite appetizers, perfect for parties and gatherings. To add color and texture, you can add two-inch pieces of steamed asparagus to each roll. 16 servings.*

1 (8-oz.) pkg. cream cheese, softened
¼ cup butter, melted
1 Tbsp. dried parsley leaves
1 clove garlic, crushed
¼ tsp. black pepper
dash of hot sauce
½ lb. deli ham

1. **Combine** all ingredients except ham in bowl.

2. **Whisk** until smooth.

3. **Spread** 1 tablespoon of mixture onto a piece of deli ham and roll.

4. **Cut** cheese-filled ham rolls into bite-sized pieces.

5. **Poke** with a frilly toothpick to secure, and serve.

Shauna Evans

Pumpkin Cheese Ball

As much as I love savory cheese balls, this is a great, sweet counterpart to the traditional. Pumpkin, chocolate, and graham crackers are an awesome trio. 16 servings.

1 (8-oz.) pkg. cream cheese, slightly softened
½ cup spiced pumpkin purée
1 tsp. vanilla extract
½ tsp. ground cinnamon
½ tsp. ground nutmeg
½ cup brown sugar
1½ cups milk chocolate chips (divided)
graham crackers for serving

1. **In a medium bowl,** combine all ingredients except 1 cup chocolate chips and graham crackers.

2. **Chill** in refrigerator for 2 hours.

3. **Form** ball and roll in reserved chocolate chips.

4. **Serve** with graham crackers.

14

Shauna Evans

Pumpkin Fruit Dip

This is one of my favorite fruit dips, especially in the fall. It's not a dip that people generally make, and it's filled with the flavors of the season. Serve with sliced apples, bananas, graham crackers, vanilla wafers, or gingersnaps. 8 servings.

1 (8-oz.) pkg. cream cheese, softened
¾ cup pumpkin purée
3 tsp. real maple syrup
½ tsp. cinnamon
¼ cup brown sugar
⅛ tsp. nutmeg

1. Blend all ingredients in bowl.

Salsa Fresca

Homemade salsa is the bomb. It's easy, quick, and full of flavor. This recipe feeds a crowd. Serve with tortilla chips. 24 servings.

3 red bell peppers, washed and chopped
1 medium onion, chopped
1 small bunch cilantro, washed and chopped, stems removed
1 small habanero chili pepper, finely minced
½ Tbsp. crushed garlic
3 vine-ripened tomatoes, puréed in blender
1 (15-oz.) can crushed tomatoes
½ cup white wine vinegar
1½ Tbsp. cumin
1½ Tbsp. chili powder
1½ Tbsp. salt
fresh ground pepper to taste

1. **Mix** all ingredients in bowl.

Shauna Evans

Stuffed Mushrooms

This elegant little dish is sure to impress guests. If you are a mushroom lover like me, you will fall head over heels for this recipe. 8 servings.

½ cup onion, minced
1 Tbsp. dried parsley leaves
⅛ tsp. black pepper
¼ tsp. Worcestershire sauce
½ cup dried bread crumbs
½ cup butter, melted (divided use)
¼ tsp. paprika
1 cup fresh Parmesan cheese, grated
35 medium button mushrooms, washed and destemmed

1. **In bowl,** combine onion, parsley, pepper, Worcestershire sauce, bread crumbs, ¼ cup butter, paprika, and Parmesan cheese.

2. **Fill** each mushroom with 1 tablespoon of crumb mixture.

3. **Place** mushrooms on cookie sheet.

4. **Pour** ¼ cup melted butter over tops of mushrooms.

5. **Bake** at 350°F for 20 minutes.

Tip: When you return from the grocery store, remove mushrooms from plastic bag and place in paper sack so mushrooms don't "sweat" and go soggy. Store in refrigerator.

Wassail

My mom always made Wassail during the Christmas season. The aromatic spices fill the air with the scent of the holidays. Garnish with cinnamon sticks. 16 servings.

1 gallon apple juice
1 (12-oz.) can frozen lemonade concentrate
2 (12-oz.) cans frozen orange juice concentrate
3 cups water
2 tsp. ground cinnamon
1 tsp. ground cloves
1 tsp. nutmeg
1 tsp. allspice

1. **Combine** all ingredients in large stockpot.

2. **Heat** to simmering.

3. **Serve** warm.

Shauna Evans

Watermelon Lemonade

🍃 *Watermelon Lemonade is refreshment in a glass. What's more "summer" than watermelon and lemonade? This recipe marries two quintessential summer foods for liquid perfection. 8 servings.*

½ small watermelon, seeded and cubed (about 6 cups)
2 (12-oz.) cans frozen lemonade concentrate
4 cups ice-cold water
2 Tbsp. grenadine syrup (optional)

1. **Put** all ingredients into blender and purée.

2. **Chill** for an hour or more.

3. **Serve** cold, garnished with small watermelon wedges.

🍃 **Tip:** *To cut a watermelon, start by cutting the rind off both short ends. With the watermelon standing on a flat end on a plate, use a sharp knife to cut the rind from top to bottom in segments, rotating as you cut. Slice watermelon in half lengthwise. If the watermelon has seeds, scoop out strip with black seeds and discard. Finish cutting watermelon lengthwise into two-inch-long segments. Then cut segments into cubes.*

Soups, Salads, and Dressings

Asian Chicken Salad

I love the flavors of the Orient, including green onions, sesame, and soy sauce. This is a beautiful salad with a perfect blend of Asian seasonings. 12 servings.

3 cups cubed cooked chicken breasts
  (or may use the meat from one cooked rotisserie chicken)
1 head green cabbage, thinly shredded
½ cup finely chopped red bell pepper
1 bunch green onion, finely chopped
½ cup slivered almonds
⅛ cup sesame seeds
2 (3-oz.) pkgs. chicken-flavored ramen noodles, uncooked and crushed (reserve seasoning packets for dressing)

1. **In large salad bowl,** combine all ingredients.

2. **Make** Asian Dressing (recipe follows).

3. **Pour** dressing over salad mixture.

4. **Refrigerate** for 1 hour before serving.

Shauna Evans

Asian Dressing

¾ cup canola oil

¼ cup sugar

3 Tbsp. soy sauce

2 Tbsp. rice vinegar

½ tsp. sesame oil

2 chicken-flavored ramen noodle dry seasoning packets

1 tsp. dry mustard

¼ tsp. black pepper

1. **In quart jar** with lid, combine ingredients and shake to blend.

2. **Chill** for 1 hour before serving.

Bleu Cheese Lettuce Wedge

I confess, I am a huge fan of Ruth's Chris Steak House. It is one of those restaurants that impresses my palate every time I dine there. This salad is my rendition of their fabulous lettuce wedge. The secret to this dish is the homemade dressing. 4 servings.

  2 cups spring greens
  1 head iceberg lettuce, cut into 4 wedges
  4 strips bacon, cooked and crumbled
  ½ cup bleu cheese

1. **Spread** ½ cup spring greens on each of 4 plates.

2. **Top** each set of greens with 1 lettuce wedge.

3. **Sprinkle** bacon pieces and ⅛ cup bleu cheese around each lettuce wedge.

4. **Top** with ¼ cup Bleu Cheese Dressing (recipe follows).

Shauna Evans

Bleu Cheese Dressing

½ cup mayonnaise
½ cup sour cream
2 Tbsp. fresh parsley, chopped fine
2 Tbsp. vinegar
1½ tsp. onion, minced
1½ tsp. fresh lemon juice
salt and pepper to taste
pinch of garlic powder
3 oz. bleu cheese, crumbled

1. **Thoroughly** combine all ingredients except bleu cheese in blender.

2. **Fold** in bleu cheese and place dressing in airtight container.

3. **Refrigerate** until ready to use.

Broccoli Salad

This salad is one of my all-time favorites. Did you know that broccoli is America's favorite vegetable? It makes perfect sense that broccoli salad is a favorite deli dish and potluck recipe. Making this salad fresh at home brings out the best flavor. It is a little sweet and a little savory—the best combination! 8 servings.

4 cups broccoli, florets washed, and cut into chunky pieces
8 slices bacon, cooked crisp and crumbled
½ cup dried cranberries
½ cup finely chopped red onion
¼ cup raw sunflower seeds, shelled
1 cup salad dressing spread (Miracle Whip)
3 Tbsp. sugar
2 Tbsp. white wine vinegar

1. **In large salad bowl,** combine broccoli, bacon, cranberries, onion, and sunflower seeds.

2. **In small mixing bowl,** whisk salad dressing spread, sugar, and vinegar for dressing.

3. **Pour** dressing over broccoli and stir to coat all broccoli pieces.

4. **Refrigerate** for 1 hour to allow flavors to develop.

Shauna Evans

Cream of Zucchini Soup

I love soups that highlight vegetables from the harvest like Cream of Zucchini Soup. This is a wonderful recipe to make when your zucchini plants are in full bloom. Garnish with cheese. 8 servings.

1 Tbsp. butter
1½ lbs. zucchini, grated (skins intact)
2 medium onions, finely chopped
3 cups chicken broth
⅛ tsp. salt
½ cup half-and-half
1 cup medium cheddar cheese, grated

1. **In skillet,** melt butter. Then add zucchini and onion. Sauté until tender.

2. **In large stockpot,** add zucchini, onion, and chicken broth and bring to a boil.

3. **Simmer** for 15 minutes.

4. **Add** salt.

5. **Purée** soup in blender.

6. **Return** soup to stockpot.

7. **Add** half-and-half and cheese to soup.

8. **Heat** until cheese is melted. Do not allow to boil. Serve warm.

Cauliflower Soup

My youngest son begs for this soup every Halloween. He calls it "pumpkin soup" because it has a soft, orange color and because I serve it in bread bowls, which resemble real pumpkins. Scoop out the bread from the bowl and use the chunks for dipping—this is half the fun. Savory comfort food at its finest. 12 servings.

4 cups cauliflower, chopped
1 cup carrots, chopped
1 onion, chopped
1 cup celery, chopped
3 cups chicken broth
2 Tbsp. finely chopped fresh parsley
1 tsp. dried basil leaves
¼ tsp. salt
¼ tsp. pepper
4 Tbsp. butter
4 Tbsp. flour
2 cups milk
12 oz. Velveeta cheese, cubed

1. **In large stockpot,** combine cauliflower, carrots, onion, celery, chicken broth, parsley, basil, salt, and pepper.

2. **Bring** to a boil and then simmer 20 minutes.

Shauna Evans

3. **Blend** 2 cups at a time in blender until vegetables are puréed. Place back in stockpot.

4. **In separate saucepan,** melt butter. Add flour and then milk all at once, stirring constantly until thickened.

5. **Add** milk mixture to puréed vegetables.

6. **Add** cheese and heat soup until cheese is melted.

California Salad

Not only is this salad incredibly pretty, but it also tastes fantastic. I really love this salad because it is deliciously different. I don't see beauty in bagged greens paired with a bottled dressing. This salad is "dressed" to impress with its citrus vinaigrette. My oldest daughter liked the dressing so much, she drank it. 10 servings.

1 head green leaf lettuce, washed and chopped

1 head red leaf lettuce, washed and chopped

1 cup fresh mushrooms, washed and sliced

1 avocado, peeled and sliced

1 cucumber, peeled and sliced

1 (7-oz.) can mandarin oranges, drained

1 small red onion, sliced thin

1. **In large salad bowl,** toss all ingredients.

2. **When** ready to serve, toss with California Citrus Dressing (recipe follows).

Tip: When cutting an avocado, score the avocado with a paring knife lengthwise along the perimeter. Pull the two sections apart. Remove the seed. Using a large spoon, scoop out the soft, green fruit from the skin. Cut lengthwise into strips and then by width into small pieces. An avocado is ripe when the skin will give a little when gently pressed.

Shauna Evans

California Citrus Dressing

½ cup orange juice concentrate (leave frozen)

2 Tbsp. orange zest

½ cup canola oil

2 Tbsp. white wine vinegar

2 Tbsp. fresh lemon juice

½ tsp. salt

2 Tbsp. sugar

1. **Place** all ingredients in jar with a lid.

2. **Shake** until well combined.

3. **Refrigerate** until ready to use.

Tortellini Soup

This classic soup, a contemporary version of chicken noodle soup, is a staple at our house. I love how quick it is to make. My five children love it. The Italian tortellini and oregano add a fun dimension and international flavor. This soup was an Aetna Healthy Food Fight national finalist, beating out several hundred contenders. 10 servings.

1 cup finely chopped onion

½ cup chopped celery

1 Tbsp. canola oil

6 cups water

1 chicken bouillon cube

1 rotisserie-roasted chicken, removed from bone and broken into pieces

3 (15-oz.) cans concentrated chicken broth

1 (15-oz.) can cream of chicken soup

2 cups carrots, peeled and cut into chunks

½ Tbsp. dried basil leaves

½ Tbsp. dried oregano leaves

2 cups broccoli, washed and cut into chunks

1 (8-oz.) pkg. frozen cheese tortellini

Parmesan cheese (garnish)

1. **In skillet,** sauté onion and celery in oil on medium heat until translucent.

2. **In large stock pot,** combine all ingredients except for broccoli, tortellini, and Parmesan cheese.

Shauna Evans

3. Simmer for 15 minutes.

4. Add broccoli and tortellini and cook for another 5 minutes.

5. Garnish with Parmesan cheese.

Fruit and Cookie Camp Salad

🌿 *I first experienced this recipe at girls camp. The camp cook paired this salad with a cheese and chicken quesadilla. It was a camp favorite. I shy away from refrigerated whipped topping, so I changed the recipe to include real whipped cream. You may also switch things up by adding bananas and kiwis. 8 servings.*

1 (5.1-oz.) pkg. dry vanilla pudding mix

2 cups buttermilk

1 cup whipping cream, whipped

1 (15-oz.) can large pineapple chunks, drained

1 (15-oz.) can mandarin oranges, drained

2 Fuji apples, chopped with skin intact

8 chocolate-striped cookies, broken into large pieces

1. **In large bowl,** combine all ingredients, adding cookies last.

2. **Refrigerate** for 1 hour, covered, before serving.

36

Shauna Evans

Tomatillo Ranch Dressing

Utilizing some of the best products of Mexico, this dressing is hard to leave alone. It is especially delicious on pork barbacoa salads. Even though I cook every day, I am a regular at fresh Mex cafés.

3 tomatillos, husked, washed, and cut into quarters

1 pkg. buttermilk ranch dressing mix

1 cup mayonnaise

1 cup fresh cilantro leaves, chopped

⅓ cup buttermilk

2 Tbsp. fresh lime juice

2 Tbsp. sugar

2 cloves garlic, minced

½ tsp. cumin

½ tsp. cayenne pepper

1. **In blender,** combine all ingredients.

2. **Purée** until texture is smooth.

3. **Refrigerate** for at least an hour before serving.

Tuscan Tomato and Corn Chowder

❧ I dream of Tuscany! When I need a taste of Italy, I make this soup. It's a snap to make and really good with grilled cheese sandwiches or crostini. Yum! 4 servings.

1 (15-oz.) can hearty tomato soup

1 (15-oz.) can creamed corn

¼ cup whipping cream

5–6 drops Mongolian fire oil (found in Asian section of supermarket)

¼ cup fresh chopped basil for garnish

1. **In saucepan,** combine first 4 ingredients.

2. **Heat through,** about 5 minutes.

3. **Garnish** with basil.

Southwest Tortilla Soup

⚬ I simply adore ethnic cuisine. So many countries have the corner on spices and seasoning. Experiencing new flavors through international foods really is enjoyable. Tortilla soup is far from foreign to many of us, however, since it hails from the Southwest. 8 servings.

½ white onion, diced
3 cloves garlic, crushed
1 (32-oz.) can crushed tomatoes
3 cups chicken broth
½ cup enchilada sauce
½ cup chopped green chilies
¼ tsp. cumin
dash of salt and pepper
2 chicken breasts, cooked and cut into pieces
4 oz. Monterey Jack cheese, shredded
2 avocados, peeled and sliced
tortilla chips

1. **In large stockpot,** combine onion, garlic, tomatoes, broth, enchilada sauce, chilies, cumin, and salt and pepper.

2. **Cook** on medium heat for 20 minutes.

3. **Let** cool for 10 minutes.

40

Shauna Evans

4. **Purée** soup in blender.

5. **Divide** chicken and cheese among 4 serving bowls. Ladle soup over top.

6. **Top** with avocados and tortilla chips.

Spring Spinach Salad

This salad is so gorgeous that it really should be photographed. What a wonderful way to celebrate spring and new life—a salad bursting with the colors, fruits, and vegetables of the season. Drizzle on a light, satisfying dressing for the finishing touch. 8 servings.

3 Tbsp. sugar
½ cup crushed almonds
1 bunch spinach leaves, washed and dried
1 cup sliced strawberries
½ red onion, sliced thin
1 (7-oz.) can mandarin oranges, drained
Spring Poppy Seed Dressing (page 44)

1. **In skillet,** melt sugar on medium heat.

2. **When** sugar starts to melt, add almonds.

3. **Remove** almonds from heat when coated with sugar.

4. **In large salad bowl,** combine spinach, strawberries, onion, and oranges.

5. **Just before serving,** sprinkle salad with almonds.

6. **Toss** with dressing.

42

Shauna Evans

Spring Poppy Seed Dressing

✎ *I recommend Spring Poppy Seed Dressing on Spring Spinach Salad (page 42). This vinaigrette is tangy, sweet, and light.*

　¾ cup canola oil
　⅓ cup sugar
　⅓ cup red wine vinegar
　¾ tsp. salt
　1 tsp. dry mustard
　1 Tbsp. poppy seeds

1. **Combine** all ingredients in quart jar with lid.

2. **Shake** to blend.

3. **Store** in refrigerator.

Shauna Evans

Mandarin Salad Dressing

Here is a simple recipe to pour over your favorite green or spinach salad instead of going for the bottled ranch dressing again.

¼ cup apple cider vinegar
2 tsp. mandarin orange juice from can
2 tsp. brown sugar
2 Tbsp. Dijon mustard
½ cup canola oil

1. **Mix** all ingredients in quart jar with lid.
2. **Chill** in refrigerator until ready to use.

Tortilla Soup

Tortilla Soup is something I could eat every day in the cool weather months. It is savory goodness in a bowl. Serve with tortilla chips, avocados, and cilantro sprigs. 12 servings.

1 Tbsp. canola oil
1 medium onion, diced
1 clove garlic, crushed
1 jalapeño pepper, seeded and minced
2 (15-oz.) cans chicken broth
3 cups grilled chicken, diced
1 (15-oz.) can stewed tomatoes with lime and green chilies
1 (15-oz.) can corn, drained
1 (15-oz.) can black beans, drained
3 Tbsp. fresh cilantro, chopped
1 Tbsp. ground cumin
1 Tbsp. fresh lime juice
dash of salt and pepper

1. **In sauté pan,** heat oil, onion, garlic, and jalapeño pepper. Cook until tender.

2. **In large stock pot,** transfer onion mixture and add all remaining ingredients.

3. **Simmer** for 15 minutes.

Touchdown Taco Soup

For two decades, we have been making this soup on game day. My father coached football in Utah and Idaho for nearly fifty years. Game day is a busy and exciting event at our home—we need something yummy and quick that feeds a crowd. This is our go-to soup with winning taste! Serve with sour cream, tortilla chips, shredded cheese, and avocado slices. 16 servings.

1 onion, diced
1 Tbsp. canola oil
1 lb. lean ground beef, browned
2 (15-oz.) cans Mexican stewed tomatoes
1 (15-oz.) can diced tomatoes with chipotles
1 (15-oz.) can tomato sauce
1 (15-oz.) can kidney beans, undrained
1 (15-oz.) can black beans, undrained
1 (15-oz.) can green beans, drained
1 (1.5-oz.) packet dry taco seasoning mix
3 cups water

1. **In pan,** cook onion in canola oil until tender.

2. **In large stockpot,** combine all ingredients.

3. **Simmer** for 15–20 minutes.

48

Shauna Evans

· · · · · · ·

Side
Dishes

· · · · · · ·

Cancun Grilled Corn

My hunky husband and I celebrated our fifteenth wedding anniversary in Cancun, Mexico. We toured ancient Mayan ruins, splashed in the ocean, and ate grilled corn from a street vendor. This recipe takes me back each time I make it. Grilled corn is one of our summer favorites! 8 servings.

8 ears fresh corn on the cob, husks intact
½ cup mayonnaise
1 (1.5-oz.) packet dry taco seasoning mix
½ cup queso blanco (white Mexican cheese) or feta cheese, finely crumbled
½ cup fresh cilantro leaves, chopped fine
4 limes, halved

1. **Boil** corn in husks for 8 minutes.

2. **Peel** husks away from corn, leaving husks attached, and grill until charred marks are on all sides, about 3 minutes. Remove corn from heat and place on serving plate.

3. **Spread** 1 tablespoon mayonnaise, 1 teaspoon taco seasoning, 1 tablespoon cheese, and 1 tablespoon cilantro on each ear of corn.

4. **Serve** with lime wedge. Squeeze lime over corn before eating.

Christmas Cranberry Salad

Christmas fare calls for cranberry recipes, as far as I am concerned. This is one of the best. The different textures and complementary flavors make this salad a standout. Bonus: It is quick and pretty at a busy time of year. It's great for family gatherings and as a side dish for Christmas dinner. 8 servings.

2 cups fresh cranberries, ground in blender

3 cups miniature marshmallows

¾ cup sugar

2 cups diced Fuji apples, skin intact

½ cup walnuts, crushed

¼ tsp. salt

1 cup whipping cream, whipped

1. **In large bowl,** fold all ingredients together.

2. **Cover** and chill for several hours or overnight.

Shauna Evans

Creamed Corn

"This corn is like an angel." –Dan in Real Life

Instead of just buttering your corn, try this simple and easy rendition for creamed corn. It is so tasty! 6 servings.

> 5 ears fresh corn or 1 (16-oz.) pkg. frozen corn kernels
> ⅓ cup whipping cream
> 1 Tbsp. sugar
> 1 Tbsp. onion, grated fine
> 2 tsp. ground nutmeg
> dash of salt and pepper

1. **Cut** corn kernels from cob.

2. **In pan over medium heat,** boil corn in a small amount of water until cooked through, about 7 minutes.

3. **Drain** water completely.

4. **Add** cream, sugar, onion, nutmeg, and salt and pepper.

5. **Heat** for 3 more minutes on medium to low heat.

Shauna Evans

German Summer Salad

This tangy bean salad is great! Don't forgo the balsamic vinegar. 12 servings.

1 (15-oz.) can kidney beans, rinsed and drained
1 (15-oz.) can corn, rinsed and drained
2 Roma tomatoes, seeded and chopped
½ green bell pepper, seeded and chopped
2–3 Tbsp. balsamic vinegar
1 Tbsp. extra virgin olive oil
½ tsp. salt
½ tsp. fresh ground black pepper

1. **In medium bowl,** combine all ingredients.

2. **Refrigerate** for 1 hour before serving.

Creamy German Slaw

With my German ancestry, I often cook German recipes. This is another welcome side dish that goes well with many main dishes. It is particularly good paired with barbecue spareribs. 12 servings.

1 small green cabbage, shredded
3 large carrots, peeled and shredded
6 radishes, shredded
⅔ cups salad dressing spread
3 Tbsp. canola oil
⅓ cup sugar
2 Tbsp. white wine vinegar
½ tsp. dry mustard
½ tsp. celery seed
½ tsp. salt

1. **In large bowl,** toss cabbage, carrots, and radishes.
2. **In a medium bowl,** combine remaining ingredients for the dressing.
3. **Pour dressing** over cabbage mixture and toss to coat.
4. **Refrigerate** for 1 hour before serving.

Side Dishes

Grandma's German Potato Salad

My late grandmother immigrated from East Germany. She was an indentured servant and worked as a nanny, cook, and housekeeper to pay off her passage to America. She was an excellent and instinctive cook who did not write down her recipes. This is as close as we could get to her famous potato salad. Hands down, this is the best potato salad I have ever tasted. 16 servings.

5 lbs. potatoes, peeled and cooked until tender
½ lb. bacon, cooked and crumbled
6 eggs, boiled and chopped into large chunks
¾ cup dill pickles, chopped
½ cup green onions, chopped
1 tsp. bacon grease
1 cup salad dressing spread
¼ cup prepared mustard
boiled eggs, sliced (garnish)

1. **In large bowl,** fold together potatoes, bacon, eggs, pickles, onions, and bacon grease.

2. **In separate bowl,** combine salad spread and mustard.

3. **Pour** sauce over potato salad and carefully stir until all potatoes are coated.

4. **Chill** for 1 hour and serve.

5. **Garnish** with sliced boiled eggs.

Shauna Evans

Orchard Applesauce

❧ Homemade applesauce is so fresh and delicious that it's worth the extra effort to prepare from scratch rather than popping open a can. 6 servings.

6 tart apples
juice of ½ lemon
½ cup water
¼ cup sugar
1 tsp. cinnamon

1. **Peel** and core apples. Cut into chunks.

2. **Place** apples in medium-sized saucepan and add lemon juice and water. Stir in sugar.

3. **Bring** to boil and then reduce heat to low. Cover and cook for 30 minutes or until apples are soft.

4. **Remove** from heat and add cinnamon. Stir lightly for chunky applesauce or rigorously for smooth sauce.

Side Dishes

Spanish Rice

Usually we only experience Spanish rice at our favorite Mexican restaurants. Here is your chance to make your own tasty Spanish Rice at home. It's surprisingly simple to make with dimensions of flavor. Who knew so many vegetables and good things went into this Mexican side dish? 24 servings.

1 (32-oz.) can tomatoes, crushed
1 medium onion, cut into eighths
1 green bell pepper, cut into eighths
1 cup Monterey Jack cheese, shredded
1 tsp. salt
¼ tsp. garlic salt
¼ tsp. dried oregano leaves
⅛ tsp. black pepper
2 cups quick-cooking white rice, uncooked

1. **Heat** oven to 350°F.

2. **Grease** a 2-quart baking dish.

3. **In a blender,** add all ingredients except for rice. Pulse for several cycles.

4. **In a bowl,** combine rice and tomato mixture.

5. **Pour** into prepared dish and bake for 35–40 minutes. Serve with your favorite Mexican dish.

Shauna Evans

Sweet Baby Carrots

These make it on the supper menu at least once a week because the kids love them, they are quick, and they go well with chicken, beef, and pork. 6 servings.

1 (1-lb.) bag baby carrots
1 cup water
3 Tbsp. butter
2 Tbsp. brown sugar

1. **In medium saucepan,** cook carrots in boiling water until tender.

2. **Drain** water from carrots.

3. **In same pan,** add butter and brown sugar. Stir until butter is melted.

Side Dishes

Irish Potato Pancakes

❧ Potato pancakes aren't just for breakfast. They are a super side dish. This is not something everyone makes, but it is something everyone loves! 8 servings.

4 large baking potatoes, peeled and grated
1 small onion, grated
4 egg yolks
2 Tbsp. lemon juice
1 tsp. baking powder
dash of nutmeg
salt and pepper to taste
3 Tbsp. butter
3 Tbsp. olive oil
ketchup

1. **In bowl,** combine potatoes, onion, egg yolks, lemon juice, baking powder, nutmeg, and salt and pepper. Set aside.

2. **Heat** butter and oil in skillet over medium heat.

3. **Drop** ¼ cup potato mixture onto hot skillet and brown on each side, for 8–10 minutes, until potato pancakes are golden and tender, turning once.

4. **Serve** with ketchup.

Shauna Evans

Pan-Seared Brussels Sprouts with Aioli Sauce

🍃 *I think Brussels sprouts are a delightful vegetable when prepared properly. This vegetable needs a little dressing up, but once outfitted with the right seasonings and sauce, it's a super star! 4 servings.*

2 cups small Brussels sprouts (look for
   tightly closed sprouts without brown wilting)
8 fresh garlic cloves, peeled (divided use)
2 Tbsp. butter
⅔ cup + 2 Tbsp. extra virgin olive oil
2 Tbsp. Parmesan cheese, shredded
2 Tbsp. fresh lemon juice
2 egg yolks
4 oz. cream cheese, softened
2 pinches sea salt
2 pinches fresh black pepper

1. **Cut** off bottom of Brussels sprouts and cut into halves.

2. **Sear** Brussels sprouts and 4 garlic cloves in butter and 2 tablespoons olive oil on medium heat in skillet for 10 minutes or until sprouts are tender and golden. Turn while cooking.

Shauna Evans

3. Transfer Brussels sprouts and garlic to serving dish and sprinkle with Parmesan cheese.

4. Make aioli sauce: In blender, combine 4 cloves garlic, lemon juice, egg yolks, cream cheese, ⅔ cup olive oil, and pinches of salt and pepper. Pulse until smooth.

5. Serve Brussels sprouts with aioli sauce.

✎ **Tip:** *While still in their paper-thin skin, crush garlic using the bottom of a drinking glass or can of food. The skin will easily pull away from the garlic and voilà: peeled garlic cloves.*

Roasted Potato Wedges and Dipping Sauce

🍂 Move over French fries—roasted potato wedges are here. These are fabulous with home-grilled hamburgers or mini meat loaves. When served with pink or white sauce, these spuds go fast. 6 servings.

5 baking potatoes, scrubbed clean and dried
¼ cup olive oil
½ Tbsp. seasoned salt

1. **Cut** each potato into 8 wedges lengthwise.

2. **Toss** potatoes with oil.

3. **Add** seasoned salt and toss again.

4. **Lay** potato wedges on cookie sheet, single layer.

5. **Bake** in 450°F oven for 40 minutes, turning potatoes after 20 minutes.

6. **Serve** with pink or white sauce (recipes follow).

Shauna Evans

Pink Sauce

1 cup ketchup
½ cup mayonnaise
1 tsp. malt vinegar

1. **In small bowl,** combine ingredients.
2. **Serve** with Roasted Potato Wedges.

White Sauce

½ cup mayonnaise
½ cup plain yogurt

1. **In small bowl,** combine
   ingredients.
2. **Serve** with Roasted Potato
   Wedges.

Toasted Garlic Broccoli

This is another side dish that is often part of our meals. My family loves it, and I love it when my kids eat their greens! It's a win-win. 6 servings.

2 Tbsp. butter
2 cloves garlic, crushed
3 cups broccoli florets
1 Tbsp. chicken broth
1 tsp. salad supreme seasoning
dash of salt and pepper
¼ cup fresh Parmesan cheese, shredded

1. **Heat** butter in medium saucepan. Add garlic and cook until toasted brown.

2. **Add** broccoli, broth, salad seasoning, and salt and pepper. Cook until broccoli is crisp and tender, about 5 minutes.

3. **Sprinkle** Parmesan cheese over hot broccoli and serve.

Spring Rolls

In 1992, I traveled to Kyoto, Japan. While there, I marveled at the sights, sounds, and some of the cuisine. Spring rolls are some of my favorite appetizers. I love the crispy texture and tender, sautéed vegetables. This variety is particularly healthy and light. Add a sweet and sour sauce for this dish to really shine. 8 servings.

1 cup frozen corn
1 cup bean sprouts
1 cup peeled and shredded carrots
1 cup frozen green beans
1 cup shredded green cabbage
1 cup edamame
¼ tsp. salt
¼ tsp. black pepper
8 spring roll wrappers
⅛ cup peanut oil

1. **In steam pan** over boiling water, steam corn, sprouts, carrots, green beans, cabbage, and edamame until tender and colorful, about 3 minutes. Remove to bowl.

2. **Sprinkle** salt and pepper on vegetable mixture.

3. **Scoop** ⅔ cup vegetable mixture into center of each wrapper set on the diagonal.

70

4. **Fold** up bottom, sides, and then top of each wrapper.

5. **Warm** peanut oil in skillet on medium heat.

6. **Brown** each spring roll in oil until golden brown on each side, about 2 minutes.

Sweet Potato Casserole

⬥ Believe it or not, Sweet Potato Casserole is not just for Thanksgiving. I cook sweet potatoes all year. They are especially yummy with steak! 16 servings.

5–6 sweet potatoes (skin left intact for cooking)

¾ cup sugar

¾ cup butter, melted (divided use)

2 eggs

1 tsp. vanilla extract

½ tsp. salt

½ cup flour

½ cup brown sugar

1 cup pecans, chopped

1. **In large stock pot**, boil sweet potatoes until tender.

2. **Wait** for them to cool before peeling.

3. **Mash** potatoes. Spread into buttered 9 × 13 baking dish.

4. **In bowl,** combine sugar, ½ cup butter, eggs, vanilla, and salt. Add to potatoes and blend.

5. **Make topping:** In a bowl, combine flour, brown sugar, ¼ cup melted butter, and pecans. Mixture should be crumbly.

Shauna Evans

6. Evenly spread pecan topping over potatoes.

7. Bake at 350°F for 40 minutes.

ɔ꞊ **Tip:** *Leave the skins on the sweet potatoes while boiling. After they have cooled, the skin will slip off easily.*

Main
Dishes

Asian Chicken

I am one of those home cooks that grills year-round—even in the dead of winter. It saves washing dishes. It is a quick form of cooking, and I love the taste of barbecue. Asian Chicken has great flavor. Serve over cooked white rice with soy sauce. Add fortune cookies and your children will think it's a party! 6 servings.

6 chicken breasts
½ cup peanut oil
½ cup soy sauce
¼ cup rice wine vinegar
2 Tbsp. sugar
1 tsp. fresh grated ginger
1 tsp. garlic, crushed
¼ cup green onions, finely chopped

1. **Place** chicken in shallow, baking dish.

2. **Mix** remaining ingredients in bowl and pour over chicken.

3. **Marinate** for 3 hours.

4. **Discard** marinade and grill chicken over medium coals for 18–20 minutes or until no longer pink.

Shauna Evans

Cashew and Chicken Salad Croissants

I think this is one of the greatest classic luncheon foods of all time. Chicken salad with cashews on a croissant has winning taste with a sophisticated flair. 6 servings.

2 cups cubed cooked chicken breasts
1 cup celery, chopped
1 bunch green onions, sliced
1 cup mayonnaise
½ tsp. dried ranch dressing mix
¼ tsp. black pepper
1 cup salted cashews
6 croissant rolls, split in half

1. **In bowl,** toss chicken, celery, and green onions. Set aside.

2. **In separate bowl**, combine mayonnaise, ranch mix, and pepper.

3. **Add** mayonnaise mixture to chicken mixture and stir to coat.

4. **Add** cashews before spooning chicken salad onto split croissants.

Shauna Evans

Giant Caesar Sandwich

If you have a luncheon to prepare for, consider making Giant Caesar Sandwiches. I have made these for my book group, and they are fabulous. They are so easy to make but are packed with flavor. Fruit salads, pickles, and potato chips go great with this dish. 8 servings.

1 round focaccia bread loaf (about 12 inches in diameter)
½ cup creamy Caesar salad dressing
½ lb. hickory-smoked, deli turkey slices
¼ lb. provolone cheese slices
5 romaine lettuce leaves, washed and dried
2 tomatoes, washed and sliced

1. **Cut** bread horizontally, making two rounds.

2. **Drizzle** dressing evenly over open rounds.

3. **Layer** meat, cheese, lettuce, and tomatoes over bottom round.

4. **Add** top half of focaccia bread.

5. **Wrap** securely in plastic wrap and refrigerate up to 4 hours.

6. **Cut** round into 8 wedges before serving.

Main Dishes

Beef Soft Tacos

These savory tacos are easy to make with pantry-friendly ingredients. Plus, tacos are a kid favorite! 12 servings.

½ cup finely chopped onion

1 clove garlic, crushed

1 Tbsp. canola oil

1½ lbs. lean ground beef, browned

1½ cups picante salsa

1 Tbsp. chili powder

2 tsp. ground cumin

½ tsp. salt

1 cup canned black beans, rinsed and drained

12 flour tortillas

Toppings

1 head romaine lettuce, washed and chopped

2 cups Monterey Jack cheese

1 avocado, sliced

2 tomatoes, sliced

1 cup sour cream

½ cup green onions, thinly sliced

Shauna Evans

1. **In skillet,** cook chopped onion and garlic in canola oil over medium heat.

2. **Add** ground beef, salsa, chili powder, cumin, salt, and beans.

3. **Simmer** for 10 minutes.

4. **Divide** taco meat among tortillas and add favorite toppings.

Chili Quick

When you're in a pinch, make Chili Quick. It's hearty and yummy. Serve with tortilla chips, grated cheese, and sour cream. 8 servings.

1 Tbsp. canola oil
1 onion, diced
½ green bell pepper, diced
1 clove garlic, minced
1 lb. lean ground beef, browned
2 (15-oz.) cans kidney beans
2 (15-oz.) cans stewed tomatoes
½ tsp. red wine vinegar
1 tsp. brown sugar
1 Tbsp. chili powder
½ Tbsp. ground cumin
dash of salt and pepper

1. **In skillet,** heat oil, onion, pepper, and garlic until tender.
2. **In medium stockpot,** add onion mixture, beef, beans, tomatoes, vinegar, brown sugar, and seasonings.
3. **Simmer** for 15 minutes.

Shauna Evans

Indian Chicken

Indian cuisine is incredible because of its variety of spices. This recipe is no different; the use of spices we don't normally throw together gives this a delicious and interesting flavor. 8 servings.

4 chicken breasts, cut into 1½-inch pieces
1 Tbsp. canola oil
1 clove garlic, crushed
¾ cup finely chopped onion
½ green bell pepper, cored, seeded, and chopped
1 Tbsp. finely chopped jalapeño pepper
1 (15-oz.) can coconut milk
1 Tbsp. cornstarch
½ tsp. each: salt, coriander, cumin, ginger, cloves, cinnamon, cardamom, black
    pepper, and dried basil
¼ tsp. each: chili powder, turmeric, cayenne pepper
½ cup shredded coconut

1. **In hot skillet,** sauté chicken in oil to brown, about 6 minutes, turning once.

2. **Turn** heat down to medium-low and add garlic, onion, and peppers to chicken. Cook until chicken is no longer pink and juices run clear, about 10 minutes.

3. **In small bowl,** mix coconut milk and cornstarch. Add coconut milk mixture and spices to chicken.

4. **Simmer** for 10 minutes more. Garnish with coconut.

83

Catalina Taco Salad

My mom would often make this for her Ladybug Club. The ladies raved about it. Later in life, I fell in love with it too. It is a little bit sweet and a little bit savory. 10 servings.

1 lb. lean ground beef, browned
2 cups mild cheddar cheese, grated
1 head romaine lettuce, washed and broken into medium-sized pieces
1 bunch green onions, diced
3 ripe tomatoes, cut into small pieces
2 cups cheese-flavored tortilla chips
1 (8-oz.) bottle Catalina salad dressing

1. **If serving** immediately, combine all ingredients in large salad bowl and toss.

2. **If not** serving immediately, combine all ingredients except for chips and dressing. Cover and chill. Add chips and dressing to individual serving bowls when prepared to serve.

Shauna Evans

Cranberry Savory Chicken

❧ Just about any recipe that incorporates sweet and savory appeals to me. This is one such recipe. The cranberries add a little sweetness, and the soup mix definitely lends a savory flavor. 8 servings.

    4 chicken breasts, cut into halves
    1 (15-oz.) can whole cranberry sauce
    1 (8-oz.) bottle French salad dressing
    1 (1.5-oz.) pkg. dry onion soup mix

1. **Place** chicken in 9 × 13 baking dish.

2. **In medium bowl,** combine cranberry sauce, dressing, and soup mix.

3. **Pour** mixture over chicken.

4. **Bake** in 350°F oven for 45–50 minutes or until chicken is no longer pink.

Shauna Evans

Citrus Tarragon Salmon

🍃 *Citrus and tarragon are perfect together—they complement salmon especially well. 4 servings.*

¼ cup fresh-squeezed lemon juice
¼ cup fresh-squeezed orange juice
1 Tbsp. white wine vinegar
1 Tbsp. extra virgin olive oil
2 tsp. orange zest
1 tsp. dried tarragon leaves
¼ tsp. salt
⅛ tsp. black pepper
4 salmon portions

1. **In a bowl,** combine citrus juices, vinegar, oil, zest, tarragon, salt, and pepper.

2. **Place** salmon in nonmetal dish. Pour citrus marinade over fish. Cover and refrigerate for 1 hour, turning once.

3. **Drain** marinade and place salmon on greased grill rack over medium coals.

4. **Grill** for 4 minutes on each side or until salmon flakes with fork.

Chicken Flautas

When we eat at fresh Mex restaurants, my husband always orders chicken flautas if they are on the menu. After dining at the delicious Loco Lizard in Park City, Utah, I was inspired to create this recipe that is easy to make and is now a family favorite. I often use a rotisserie chicken to prepare this dish when I am in a time crunch—which is often, with five active children involved in music and sports. 8 servings.

4 oz. cream cheese, softened
½ cup chipotle mayonnaise
8 (10-inch) fresh flour tortillas
2 cups cooked chicken, shredded
½ cup feta cheese, crumbled
1 Tbsp. canola oil for browning
2 cups hot pepper jelly (use a quality brand)
½ cup cilantro sprigs, washed

1. **Spread** 1 tablespoon cream cheese followed by 1 tablespoon chipotle mayonnaise on each flour tortilla.

2. **Spread** ¼ cup cooked chicken in middle of each tortilla.

3. **Sprinkle** 1 tablespoon feta cheese over chicken.

4. **Roll** up tortilla by folding in all sides.

5. **In skillet,** heat oil and brown 4 filled tortilla shells at a time until golden. Turn once.

Shauna Evans

6. Spread 1 tablespoon hot pepper jelly over the top of each flauta and sprinkle with 1 tablespoon feta cheese.

7. Serve with cilantro sprig and hot pepper jelly for dipping.

Clam Sauce over Angel-Hair Pasta

This is one of my favorite pasta dishes, and I often crave it. I love seafood, but you will find that people who don't necessarily have a penchant for fish will enjoy this sauce. 8 servings.

2 Tbsp. butter

2 Tbsp. olive oil

¾ cup onion, minced

1 clove garlic, crushed

2 Tbsp. fresh parsley, chopped fine

3 (7.5-oz.) cans chopped clams with juice

salt and pepper to taste

1 tsp. dried basil leaves

1 tsp. dried thyme leaves

1 cup whipping cream

1½ Tbsp. flour

½ cup Parmesan cheese

1 lb. angel-hair pasta, cooked tender (about 6 minutes in salted, boiling water)

1. **Heat butter** and olive oil together in skillet. Sauté onion and garlic until translucent.

2. **Add** parsley, clams with juice, and salt and pepper.

Shauna Evans

3. Add basil, thyme, cream, flour, and Parmesan cheese. Simmer 15 minutes. Do not allow to boil.

4. Serve over angel-hair pasta.

Main Dishes

General Watts's Favorite Barbecue Spareribs

✎ Maurice Watts was the general of Utah's National Guard for decades. He is my aunt's late father-in-law. This was his favorite recipe. Once you taste it, I'm sure you will understand why. The former conductor of the Utah Symphony called to thank me for sharing this recipe with his wife. I guess you could say it was music to his mouth. 12 servings.

2 Tbsp. butter

2 Tbsp. canola oil

6 lbs. boneless, country-style pork spareribs

salt and pepper to taste

1 (12-oz.) bottle ketchup

½ cup brown sugar

¼ cup Worcestershire sauce

¼ cup apple cider vinegar

1 Tbsp. prepared mustard

1. **In skillet,** melt butter and heat oil on medium heat. Add spareribs sprinkled with salt and pepper. Brown on all sides.

2. **Transfer** ribs and drippings to large stockpot or slow cooker.

3. **Make** barbecue sauce by combining ketchup, sugar, Worcestershire sauce, vinegar, and mustard. Pour over ribs in pot.

4. **Cook** ribs on medium-low heat for 3–4 hours or until ribs fall apart with fork.

Shauna Evans

Fettuccine Alfredo

Here is a classic white sauce. If you like Alfredo, you'll love this recipe. I love to pair a white sauce with a red sauce. When the two sauces mingle on a plate, it's pasta magic—heaven, really! 6 servings.

1 (8-oz.) pkg. Neufchâtel or cream cheese, softened
1 cup finely shredded fresh Parmesan cheese (divided use)
½ cup butter
⅔ cup low-fat milk
¼ tsp. garlic powder
dash of salt
8 oz. fettuccine noodles, cooked tender

1. **In a large saucepan,** stir together Neufchâtel or cream cheese, ¾ cup Parmesan cheese, butter, milk, garlic powder, and salt until smooth.

2. **Pour** over noodles and top with remaining Parmesan cheese.

Creamy Herb Chicken Tetrazzini

This recipe won the B98.7 radio station recipe contest in February 2011. This wonderful, savory dish is sure to win you over as well. 8 servings.

4 chicken breasts, cut into 1½-inch cubes
1 Tbsp. olive oil
1 Tbsp. butter
½ cup finely chopped onion
2 cups half-and-half
2 Tbsp. Savory Herb with Garlic dry soup mix
½ cup button mushrooms, washed and sliced
½ cup frozen peas, thawed under cool water
1 lb. linguine noodles, cooked tender (about 9 minutes in boiling, salted water)
fresh parsley for garnish
Parmesan cheese, finely shredded (garnish)

1. **In skillet** on medium heat, brown chicken in olive oil and butter on all sides, about 6 minutes.

2. **Add** onion and cook for another 5 minutes on medium-low heat.

3. **Add** half-and-half and dry soup mix and simmer for 10 minutes.

Shauna Evans

4. Add mushrooms and peas and warm through, about 3 minutes.

5. Serve chicken over cooked linguine noodles. Garnish with parsley and Parmesan cheese.

Delilah's Tacos

My maternal grandmother created this simple, savory taco. She looked and dressed like a Hollywood star but cooked, cleaned, and sewed like a 1950s quintessential homemaker. If you ask any of my five children, or the neighbors' five children, they would all say this is the number one best thing I cook. Talk about kid approved. My Grandma Delilah sure did know what she was doing, and I am grateful for it! 12 servings.

1 lb. lean ground beef, browned
1 (15-oz.) can bean with bacon soup
⅛ cup water
12 corn tortillas
½ cup canola oil

Toppings

1 bunch green onions, chopped
3 tomatoes, chopped
2 cups Monterey Jack cheese, shredded
1 head romaine lettuce, washed and chopped

1. **After** browning beef in skillet, add bean with bacon soup and water.

2. **Simmer** for 10 minutes on low heat.

Shauna Evans

3. In shallow pan, fry corn tortillas in canola oil until slightly crisp. Place cooked tortillas between paper towels to soak up extra oil.

4. Assemble tacos by dividing meat mixture and toppings among 12 corn tortillas.

Hot Chicken Salad

Here is another fantastic brunch food, but don't hesitate to make it for dinner. My kids and hubby give it two thumbs up. 8 servings.

3 cups cooked and cubed chicken breasts
⅓ cup chicken broth
2 cups chopped celery
1 (4-oz.) jar finely chopped pimentos
1 (5-oz.) can mushrooms, drained
1¼ cup mayonnaise
3 Tbsp. lemon juice
2 Tbsp. onion, grated
1 tsp. salt and pepper
8 washed lettuce leaves
1 cup potato chips, crushed

1. **In bowl,** combine all ingredients except for lettuce leaves and potato chips.

2. **Place** mixture in baking dish and bake at 375°F for 30 minutes.

3. **Spoon** ¾ cup chicken salad on each lettuce leaf and sprinkle with potato chips just before serving.

Fried Chicken

"Fried chicken just tend to make you feel better about life."

—Minny Jackson from The Help.

✎ *I do love fried chicken. You don't have to be from the South to master this recipe. This is so good and easy—really. My mom often made fried chicken for Sunday dinner. What a wonderful comfort food. 6 servings.*

6 skinless, boneless chicken breasts
1 cup flour
1 tsp. salt
1 tsp. ground pepper
1 tsp. paprika
1 tsp. garlic powder
2 Tbsp. canola oil
1 Tbsp. butter

1. **Cut** chicken breasts into 3 strips each.

2. **In a large,** paper grocery bag, add the flour, salt, pepper, paprika, and garlic powder.

3. **Add** chicken to bag, roll the top down, and shake until chicken is coated.

4. **Heat** oil and butter in skillet on medium-high heat.

5. **Add** chicken to pan and sear each side of chicken, approximately 5 minutes per side or until nice and golden brown.

100

Shauna Evans

6. Turn down heat to medium-low and continue to cook chicken until no longer pink, 10–12 minutes, turning once.

Tip: To test chicken for doneness, cut into the largest piece of chicken to see if it's no longer pink. If the largest piece is cooked through, then all the pieces will be cooked through. Do not pierce the chicken with a fork while cooking or the juices will be released and the chicken will not be moist and tender. Pan searing seals in the juices. The butter helps with the browning and the crispy outer crust.

Main Dishes

Pork Barbacoa

❧ *If you are a fan of fresh Mex food, then you are no stranger to pork barbacoa. This has got to be one of the best sweet and savory recipes known to man. 16 servings.*

2 (15-oz.) cans tomato sauce
4 cups Dr Pepper soda
½ cup brown sugar
3 Tbsp. molasses
1 Tbsp. cumin
3 tsp. garlic, crushed
1 (4-lb.) supreme, boneless pork roast

1. **Mix** all ingredients except pork in bowl.

2. **In large stockpot** or slow cooker, add roast.

3. **Pour** sauce over pork roast.

4. **Cook** for 6–7 hours on low to medium heat.

5. **Shred** pork and cook for another hour.

Shauna Evans

Mexican Kitchen Carnitas

🍃 *My parents discovered carnitas in the 1980s while eating at a delicious Mexican restaurant in New Port Beach, California, where my dad recruited for the Brigham Young University football team. When they returned from their trip, they devised how to make these at home. My four brothers and I fell in love with them. I have been making carnitas ever since. 16 servings.*

1 Tbsp. canola oil

1 Tbsp. butter

6 lbs. premium, boneless pork roast

1 tsp. salt

1 tsp. pepper

1 tsp. garlic powder

1 tsp. thyme

½ tsp. granulated sugar

2 cups water

1 (12-count) pkg. white corn tortillas

2 cups shredded Colby Jack cheese

1 cup sour cream

1 bunch cilantro leaves, washed and chopped

4 fresh limes, quartered

2 avocados, sliced

1. **Heat oil** and butter in large skillet. Add roast to skillet and seasonings to roast. Brown on all sides.

2. **Transfer** roast and all drippings to large stockpot. Add 2 cups water.

3. **Cook** roast on low on stovetop for 5–6 hours or until roast falls apart.

4. **Remove** from heat and shred pork.

5. **Warm** tortillas in microwave.

6. **Top** each tortilla with pork, cheese, sour cream, cilantro, lime juice, and avocado slices.

Mini Barbecue Meat Loaves

❧ *As a kid, I was far from enamored with meat loaf. It was a "stuffy" food to me. However, these mini meat loaves are very contemporary and flavorfully baked with a tangy barbecue sauce. They are especially good hot out of the oven with potato wedges. My kids gobble them up. 6 servings.*

1½ lbs. ground beef
¾ cup old-fashioned rolled oats
1 cup milk
3 Tbsp. onion, minced
1 Tbsp. dried parsley flakes
1½ tsp. salt
1 tsp. pepper
1 cup ketchup
2 Tbsp. sugar
3 Tbsp. apple cider vinegar
2 Tbsp. Worcestershire sauce
½ Tbsp. prepared mustard

1. **In a medium bowl,** combine ground beef, oats, milk, onion, parsley, salt, and pepper.

2. **Using hands,** form mini meat loaves using ¼ cup meat mixture for each loaf.

Shauna Evans

3. **Place** in greased 9 × 13 dish.

4. **Prepare sauce:** Combine ketchup, sugar, vinegar, Worcestershire sauce, and mustard.

5. **Pour** 1–2 tablespoons of sauce over each mini meat loaf.

6. **Bake** in 350°F oven for 40–45 minutes or until cooked through.

Mama Mia Pizza

❧ *Growing up, my family ate out maybe once a year. I know—shocking! My dad was a football coach, so home-cooked meals were the only way to keep food in the mouths of four boys and one girl. However, when my dad's team took the high school championship (five times), we went to the Pizza Oven in Salt Lake City to celebrate. This was the highlight of my year. I was fascinated as I watched the pizza makers behind glass stretching the dough and deftly applying the toppings. This recipe is my mom's earnest effort to create Pizza Oven–esque pizza for her family. 24 servings.*

1 (6-oz.) can tomato sauce

1 (6-oz.) can tomato paste

1 Tbsp. Italian seasoning

2 tsp. crushed garlic

pinch of sugar

pinch of salt

2 tsp. water

4 loaves frozen white bread dough, thawed and raised according to
    package directions

1 cup Parmesan cheese

1 lb. cheddar cheese, shredded

1 lb. mozzarella cheese, shredded

pepperoni (enough for 4 pizzas)

2 (5-oz.) cans mushrooms, drained

1 lb. sausage, browned

Shauna Evans

1. **In saucepan,** combine tomato sauce, paste, Italian seasoning, garlic, sugar, salt, and water.

2. **Simmer** sauce on low heat while preparing dough and toppings.

3. **Grease** 4 large, dark cookie sheets.

4. **Stretch** raised bread dough to fit each sheet, using fingers to form to sides.

5. **Spoon** one quarter pizza sauce over each sheet of dough.

6. **Sprinkle** ¼ Parmesan cheese over pizza sauce on each sheet.

7. **Divide** cheddar cheese, mozzarella cheese, pepperoni, mushrooms, and sausage among the sheets of dough.

8. **Cook** pizzas one at a time on bottom rack of a 400°F oven for 10–12 minutes or until crust is golden.

Mama's Spaghetti with Red Meat Sauce

My mother has been making this recipe since I was born. It is simple, family friendly, and easy. This is another recipe that my kids rank in the top ten. 12 servings.

1 lb. lean ground beef, browned
½ lb. sausage, browned
1 (32-oz.) can crushed tomatoes
1 (6-oz.) can tomato paste
1 Tbsp. dried parsley flakes
2 tsp. crushed garlic
½ tsp. black pepper
½ tsp. salt
1 Tbsp. Italian seasoning
pinch of sugar
8 oz. spaghetti noodles, cooked until tender (about 8 minutes in salted, boiling water)
Parmesan cheese (garnish)

1. **After** browning ground beef and sausage, add tomatoes, tomato paste, seasonings, and sugar. Stir to mix.

2. **Simmer** for 15 minutes.

3. **Serve** sauce over cooked spaghetti noodles. Garnish with Parmesan cheese.

110

Tip: *To cook pasta, follow package directions. Cook pasta in salted water (about 1 teaspoon salt). Put the noodles in after the water is boiling. Then boil for about 8 minutes or until al dente, or "to the tooth," meaning a noodle will be tender when bitten between your teeth. Another authentic Italian technique is to throw the noodle against the wall and if it sticks, then the pasta is done. Your kids will get a kick out of this technique.*

111

Manti Barbecue Chicken Kebabs

📯 Manti, Utah, is famous for its barbecue turkey breasts. My husband went to college in Ephraim, near Manti. He fell in love with this recipe while living there. Here is a twist on that award-winning marinade. 8 servings.

1 cup lemon-lime soda
½ cup canola oil
½ cup soy sauce
½ tsp. crushed garlic
½ tsp. horseradish
4 chicken breasts, cut into 1½-inch chunks.
8 wooden skewers
1 red onion cut into eighths
1 green bell pepper cut into eighths
24 button mushrooms, washed and destemmed

1. **For marinade,** combine soda, oil, soy sauce, garlic, and horseradish in shallow baking dish or resealable bag.

2. **Add** chicken to marinade. Let chicken marinate for at least 4 hours in refrigerator.

3. **Soak** skewers in water for 30 minutes.

Shauna Evans

4. **Thread** marinated chicken chunks on each skewer, alternating with red onion, green bell pepper, and mushrooms, leaving ¼-inch space between pieces.

5. **Grill** skewers on medium heat for about 7 minutes each side, turning once, testing largest chicken piece to make sure no longer pink.

✎ **Tip:** *Soaking the skewers in water beforehand prevents burning while grilling.*

Main Dishes

Marinated Chicken Kebabs

I love kebabs. It's a fun word to say, and they are even better to eat. Even though they are easy to make, they look impressive and fancy. They are deliciously chic. 8 servings.

¾ cup canola oil

¾ cup soy sauce

½ cup lemon juice

¼ cup Worcestershire sauce

¼ cup prepared mustard

1½ tsp. black pepper

1 tsp. garlic, crushed

4 chicken breasts, cut into 1½-inch chunks

4 skewers

1 red onion, cut into eighths

1 green bell pepper, cut into eighths

1 red bell pepper, cut into eighths

1. **For marinade,** combine first 7 ingredients in shallow, nonmetal baking dish.

2. **Add** chicken to marinade. Cover and allow to sit in refrigerator for 3–4 hours.

3. **Soak** skewers in water for 30 minutes.

4. **Remove** meat from marinade.

Shauna Evans

5. Thread meat, alternating with onion and peppers, on skewers, leaving ¼-inch space between pieces.

6. Grill on medium coals for 8–10 minutes, turning once, until chicken is no longer pink.

Sugar and Spice Steaks

This is one of my favorite ways to prepare grilled steak. 8 servings.

3 tsp. salt
3 tsp. black pepper
1½ tsp. garlic powder
7 tsp. sugar
4 (1-lb.) top sirloin steaks, about 1 inch thick

1. **In small bowl,** combine salt, pepper, garlic powder, and sugar.

2. **Rub** both sides of steaks with sugar and spice rub.

3. **Let** sit at room temperature for 20 minutes.

4. **Grill** steak over medium-hot coals, 5 minutes on each side for medium rare.

5. **Carve** diagonally in ¼-inch slices.

Sweet and Sour Chicken

𝒮 Sweet and Sour Chicken is a fun way to prepare poultry. It is light and tastes great with cooked rice. 6 servings.

3 lbs. chicken breasts, cut into 1½-inch chunks

1 tsp. garlic salt

½ tsp. ground black pepper

1 (15-oz.) can large pineapple chunks, drained

1 green bell pepper, seeded and cut into 1-inch chunks

½ cup sugar

½ cup apple cider vinegar

½ cup chicken broth

3½ Tbsp. ketchup

1 Tbsp. soy sauce

1. **Place** chicken in 9 × 13 baking dish. Sprinkle with salt and pepper. Add pineapple and green bell pepper chunks.

2. **Make sauce:** In small bowl, combine sugar, vinegar, broth, ketchup, and soy sauce.

3. **Pour** sauce over chicken.

4. **Cook** chicken uncovered in a 325°F oven for 45 minutes or until no longer pink.

Shauna Evans

Yogurt Chicken

The yogurt in this chicken recipe makes it very moist. The crackers give it a buttery, golden crust. 6 servings.

1 pkg. butter crackers, crushed
1 tsp. garlic powder
½ tsp. salt
½ tsp. black pepper
1 cup plain yogurt
6 chicken breasts

1. **In shallow bowl,** combine crackers, garlic powder, salt, and black pepper.

2. **Spread** yogurt evenly on a plate

3. **Dip** each chicken breast in yogurt. Then dip in cracker crumbs to coat.

4. **Place** in greased 9 × 13 baking dish and bake at 350°F for 45 minutes or until chicken is cooked through.

Main Dishes

Sloppy Joes

Sloppy Joes are a country classic. They are easy to prepare and tasty. Mix things up by serving them open faced or on toasted sourdough rolls. This is a fun food for cowboy-themed birthday parties. 6 servings.

1 clove garlic, crushed
1 cup onion, minced
1 red bell pepper, seeded and chopped
1 Tbsp. canola oil
1 lb. lean ground beef, browned
⅛ tsp. cayenne pepper
1 (32-oz.) can tomatoes, crushed
1 can tomato paste
⅔ cup ketchup
⅓ cup red wine vinegar
2 Tbsp. brown sugar
1 Tbsp. Worcestershire sauce
6 hamburger buns, toasted

1. **In skillet,** cook garlic, onion, and red bell pepper in oil over medium heat for 6 minutes.

2. **Add** browned meat and cayenne pepper. Cook for 1 minute.

Shauna Evans

3. **Stir** in tomatoes, tomato paste, ketchup, vinegar, brown sugar, and Worcestershire sauce. Stir to coat meat.

4. **Cook** on medium-low heat for 10 minutes more.

5. **Divide** sloppy joe mixture among 6 buns.

Spaghetti with Artichoke Hearts and Tomatoes

Artichoke hearts are one of those special foods that stand out beautifully in pasta recipes. This fresh pasta is quick to make, meatless, and delicious. 8 servings.

2 (6-oz.) jars marinated artichoke hearts in oil

¼ cup extra virgin olive oil

¾ cup onion, minced

2 cloves garlic, minced

½ tsp. dried oregano leaves

½ tsp. dried basil leaves

½ tsp. black pepper

½ tsp. salt

1 (32-oz.) can diced tomatoes

¼ cup Parmesan cheese, grated

¼ cup fresh parsley, chopped

⅛ cup black olives, sliced

1 lb. spaghetti, cooked until tender

1. **Separate** artichokes from marinade, reserving the oil.

2. **Heat** the olive oil and artichoke marinade in a large skillet. Add onions, garlic, oregano, basil, pepper, and salt. Cook over medium heat until onions are tender, about 8 minutes.

Shauna Evans

3. Add tomatoes and simmer for 15 minutes.

4. Add artichoke hearts, Parmesan, parsley, and olives. Simmer for another 5 minutes.

5. To serve, toss with pasta.

Sunday Pot Roast

🍃 *I am no different than many home cooks when it comes to making pot roast on Sunday. It is a hearty meal that slowly cooks while moms are busy at church with their families. I usually pair this with mashed potatoes. I forgo adding potatoes to the roast itself, because they make the meat taste "starchy." 12 servings.*

5-lb. supreme pot roast
1 tsp. salt
1 tsp. pepper
1 tsp. thyme
1 tsp. garlic powder
dash of sugar
2 Tbsp. butter
2 Tbsp. canola oil
1 cup apple juice
3 cups water
3 cups carrots, peeled and cut into coins
1 onion, sliced thin

1. **Rub** roast with all seasonings, covering all sides.

2. **In large skillet,** heat butter and canola oil. Brown roast on all sides.

3. **Transfer** roast to large stockpot.

4. **Pour** apple juice into skillet. Scrape all drippings loose from pan and pour over roast.

124

Shauna Evans

5. **Add** 3 cups water to roast.

6. **Cook** roast on low heat for 5–6 hours or until it breaks apart with fork.

7. **Add** carrots and onion the last 2 hours of cooking.

Tip: *If the roast does not fall apart when cut with a fork, then it is not done cooking. Pop it back in the oven or on the pot on the stove and continue to cook it until it does fall apart.*

Tarragon Herb Butter with Salmon Steaks

4 servings.

¼ cup butter, slightly softened
1½ tsp. fresh lemon juice
dash of black pepper
1 Tbsp. chopped fresh parsley
¼ tsp. dried tarragon
4 salmon steaks
lemon wedges

1. **In small bowl,** beat butter until fluffy. Add lemon juice, pepper, parsley, and tarragon

2. **Place** salmon steaks on a 12 × 24 sheet of tinfoil.

3. **Place** 1 tablespoon herb butter mixture over each steak.

4. **Fold** tinfoil over salmon and seal edges by rolling them.

5. **On heated grill,** cook salmon over medium-hot coals for 8–12 minutes or until salmon flakes with a fork and is no longer opaque.

6. **Serve** with lemon wedges and remaining herb butter.

Shauna Evans

Yorkshire Puddings

¼ cup canola oil
1 cup flour
¾ tsp. salt
2 eggs, beaten
1 cup milk

1. **Place** 1 teaspoon oil in each cup of a 12-muffin tin.

2. **Place** muffin tin in 400°F oven.

3. **In bowl,** sift flour and salt.

4. **In separate bowl,** combine eggs and milk.

5. **Add** dry ingredients to egg mixture and beat until smooth.

6. **Take** muffin tin out of oven.

7. **Pour** 3 tablespoons of pudding batter into each muffin cup.

8. **Return** puddings to oven and bake for 30 minutes or until puddings are golden brown.

9. **If puddings get too brown,** turn heat down to 350°F to finish baking.

10. **Serve** with Yorkshire Beef (page 128).

Main Dishes

Yorkshire Beef

❧ You will not find a better recipe for Yorkshire Beef. My mom has been making this recipe for thirty years. This is not a recipe every home cook has on hand; it is truly special. My mother tried Yorkshire beef in Spain at a restaurant near the Rock of Gibraltar. It did not fare as well as hers. 10 servings.

2 lbs. round steak
3 Tbsp. flour
2 Tbsp. canola oil
1 tsp. dried basil leaves
¼ tsp. black pepper
¾ cup water
½ cup beef broth
1 (15-oz.) can cheddar cheese soup
½ cup sliced green onions
½ cup canned mushrooms, drained

1. **Cut** steak into ¾-inch cubes.

2. **Dredge** steak pieces in flour and brown in hot oil in skillet until browned on each side, about 6 minutes.

3. **Sprinkle** basil and pepper over meat.

4. **Add** water and cover tightly. Cook slowly on low heat for 1 hour.

5. **Add** beef broth and continue cooking 30 minutes more or until meat is tender. Stir occasionally.

128

Shauna Evans

6. **Remove** ½ cup cooking liquid and combine with cheddar cheese soup. Then return to skillet.

7. **Add** green onions and mushrooms.

8. **Serve** over Yorkshire Puddings (page 127).

White Chicken Chili

This recipe received a blue ribbon from Just a Pinch Recipe Club. When most people think of chili, they think of a red, tomato-based chili with hamburger and kidney beans. Here is a unique, beautiful, and savory White Chicken Chili that will knock your wool socks off! 10 servings.

2 cloves fresh garlic, crushed

1 cup chopped onion

1 Tbsp. canola oil

1 lb. cooked chicken, cubed (or meat from a cooked rotisserie chicken)

2 (15-oz.) cans great northern beans, rinsed and drained

2 (4-oz.) cans green chilies, chopped

1 (15-oz.) can chicken broth

1 tsp. ground cumin

1 tsp. dried oregano leaves

1 tsp. salt

½ tsp. black pepper

¼ tsp. cayenne pepper

1 cup sour cream

½ cup milk

1. **In skillet,** cook garlic, onion, and oil on medium heat until translucent.

2. **In stockpot,** add onion mixture, cubed chicken, beans, chilies, broth, cumin, oregano, salt, black pepper, and cayenne pepper.

130

Shauna Evans

3. Simmer for 15 minutes and then take off heat.

4. Add sour cream and milk. Stir to combine and serve.

Tip: *If you're in a time crunch, as many busy moms are, then buy a cooked rotisserie chicken at the grocer. Remove the meat from the bones and add to your recipes calling for cooked chicken. This is often my fallback method.*

Banana Bread

♫ Kids go bananas for this bread. It's one good recipe you will want to double. Makes 1 loaf.

3 overripe bananas, peeled and mashed
1 cup brown sugar
1 egg
4 Tbsp. butter, softened
1 tsp. vanilla extract
1½ cups flour
1 tsp. baking soda
½ tsp. salt

1. **In large bowl,** combine bananas, sugar, egg, butter, and vanilla. Beat well.

2. **In separate bowl,** sift flour, baking soda, and salt.

3. **Stir** flour mixture into banana mixture just until blended.

4. **Pour** into a buttered loaf pan and bake in 325°F oven for 1 hour or until knife comes out clean.

5. **Allow** bread to sit in pan for 10 minutes before turning onto cooling rack.

Sweet Potato Muffins

This is like sweet potato casserole in muffin form. These muffins are especially moist, with wonderful spices. 12 servings.

1¼ cups + 2 Tbsp. sugar (divided use)
1¼ cups cooked and mashed yams
½ cup butter, softened
2 large eggs, room temperature
1½ cups flour
2 tsp. baking powder
½ tsp. nutmeg
¼ tsp. salt
1 cup milk
1 tsp. cinnamon

1. **Beat** 1¼ cups sugar, yams, and butter until smooth.

2. **Add** eggs and blend well.

3. **In separate bowl,** sift flour, baking powder, nutmeg, and salt.

4. **Add** dry mixture alternately with milk to yam mixture, stirring just to blend.

5. **Spoon** mixture into greased muffin tins, filling only two-thirds full. Sprinkle tops with remaining sugar mixed with cinnamon.

6. **Bake** in 400°F oven for 25–30 minutes or until toothpick comes out clean.

Shauna Evans

Carrot Muffins

I love the carrot bread from Mimi's Cafe. This is as close as I can get to that lovely recipe. 12 servings.

2 cups flour
1¼ cups sugar
2 tsp. baking soda
2 tsp. cinnamon
½ tsp. salt
2 cups peeled and shredded carrots
½ cup raisins
1 apple, peeled and diced
3 eggs
1 cup canola oil
2 tsp. vanilla extract

1. **In large bowl,** sift flour, sugar, baking soda, cinnamon, and salt.

2. **Stir** in carrots, raisins, and apple.

3. **In separate bowl,** beat eggs, oil, and vanilla.

4. **Combine** carrot mixture with egg mixture until just moistened.

5. **Spoon** batter into greased muffin tins.

6. **Bake** in 350°F oven for 20–25 minutes or until knife comes out clean.

Peach Muffins

The peach is one of my favorite fruits. This muffin recipe is good because the peaches don't just blend in—they stand out. 12 servings.

2 cups flour
⅔ cup sugar
1 tsp. baking powder
½ tsp. salt
½ tsp. cinnamon
¼ tsp. nutmeg
¾ cup milk
¼ cup butter
2 large eggs, slightly beaten
1½ cups fresh peaches, peeled and chopped, or canned

1. **In large bowl,** combine flour, sugar, baking powder, salt, cinnamon, and nutmeg.

2. **In small bowl,** stir together milk, butter, and eggs.

3. **Add** milk mixture to flour mixture. Stir just until moistened. Batter will be lumpy.

4. **Fold** in peaches.

5. **Bake** in 425°F oven for 20–25 minutes or until golden and center springs back when lightly pressed.

6. **Cool** on wire rack.

Shauna Evans

Sunday Dinner Rolls

These are the perfect rolls for Sunday because they are quick to make and satisfying. 18 servings.

3¾ cups white flour
¼ cup butter, softened
¾ cup warm milk
¼ cup sugar
2 Tbsp. yeast
½ cup water
1 egg
1 tsp. salt

1. **Combine** all ingredients in bowl.

2. **Mix** until smooth.

3. **Let** dough rise in buttered bowl for 1 hour.

4. **Divide** into 18 pieces. Form rolls by rolling a piece of dough between palm and work surface with a little pressure.

5. **Place** rolls in buttered 9 × 13 baking dish. Let rise until doubled.

6. **Bake** in 350°F oven for 13 minutes or until tops are golden brown.

Butterflake Rolls

Homemade rolls are one of my weaknesses. I have a hard time leaving freshly made rolls alone. These rolls are yummy. 24 servings.

2 Tbsp. yeast
2 cups warm water (divided use)
¾ cup + 1 Tbsp. sugar
½ cup butter
½ cup vegetable shortening
6 cups white flour
2 eggs, beaten
2 tsp. salt
1 tsp. baking powder
¼ cup melted butter

1. **Proof** yeast by sprinkling yeast over 1 cup warm water.

2. **Wait** 1 minute and then add 1 tablespoon sugar to yeast mixture.

3. **In small bowl,** melt ½ cup butter and shortening in 1 cup warm water in microwave.

4. **In large bowl,** place ¾ cup sugar. Pour butter mixture over sugar and stir until sugar is dissolved. Let cool 10 minutes.

5. **Add** 2 cups flour then 2 beaten eggs. Beat well.

6. **Mix** 1 cup flour with salt and baking powder. Add to flour and egg mixture.

140

Shauna Evans

7. **Add** yeast mixture.

8. **Gradually** add 3 cups flour, or enough that dough pulls away from bowl.

9. **Let** dough rise in buttered bowl, covered with cloth, until doubled.

10. **Punch** dough down. Divide into two balls and roll out to 12-inch circles on floured surface.

11. **Using pizza cutter,** cut circle into 12 wedges. Brush with melted butter and roll up from broad end to tip to form a crescent shape.

12. **Once shaped,** let rise a second time until doubled. Bake at 375°F for 10–15 minutes or until golden brown.

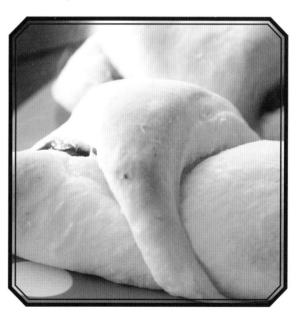

Flour Tortillas

If you have never made flour tortillas, then you will be pleasantly surprised by how easy they are to make. They taste great topped with butter and honey, or butter and cinnamon sugar, for a sweet treat. 8 servings.

> 2 cups flour
> 1 tsp. salt
> 1 tsp. baking powder
> ¼ cup shortening
> ½ cup cold water

1. **Sift** dry ingredients.

2. **Cut** in shortening.

3. **Sprinkle** water on top of flour mixture until moistened into soft, pliable dough. May need to use up to ¾ cup water.

4. **Divide** dough into 8 balls. Cover with towel and let stand 15 minutes.

5. **Roll** out to 7-inch circles.

6. **Cook** on ungreased, nonstick pan or griddle on low to medium heat until tortilla bubbles, about 30 seconds.

7. **Flip** tortilla and cook another 30 seconds.

Shauna Evans

Pizza Dough

❧ What could be more fun than making your own pizza on homemade dough? Adults and kids alike love orchestrating a pizza with their favorite toppings.

2½ cups bread flour
1 cup water
1 Tbsp. yeast
2 Tbsp. olive oil (plus more)
½ tsp. salt

1. **Mix** all ingredients together and knead for 8 minutes.

2. **Let** rest 5 minutes.

3. **Roll** out on floured surface to ⅛-inch thickness.

4. **Spread** thin layer of olive oil over dough before baking.

5. **Add** favorite toppings.

6. **Bake** at 400°F on bottom rack or outdoor grill for 10 minutes.

Charlotte's Zucchini Bread

This is my grandmother's recipe for zucchini bread. It is moist and delicious, and the pineapple gives it a fresh twist. Makes 2 loaves.

3 eggs
1 cup canola oil
1 cup sugar
2 tsp. vanilla extract
1 cup brown sugar
3 cups flour
1 tsp. allspice
2 tsp. cinnamon
½ tsp. ground cloves
1 tsp. salt
1 tsp. baking soda
¼ tsp. baking powder
2 cups zucchini, washed and grated with skin
1 (13-oz.) can crushed pineapple (draining off excess liquid)
1 cup walnuts, chopped

1. **In large bowl,** combine eggs, oil, sugar, and vanilla until fluffy.

2. **Sift** dry ingredients and add to egg mixture.

3. **Add** zucchini, pineapple, and nuts.

Shauna Evans

4. Pour into 2 greased loaf pans. Bake at 325°F for 45 minutes.

5. Cool slightly and then drizzle with Lemon Icing (recipe follows).

Lemon Icing

    1 Tbsp. butter, melted
    1 tsp. lemon juice
    ½ cup powdered sugar

1. Combine all ingredients in small bowl and drizzle over warm zucchini bread.

Honey Wheat Bread

🍃 *After I got married, my first job was at a whole wheat bakery. There I learned to knead and shape dough as well as slice bread. With that experience under my apron, I spent hours at home trying to create a recipe similar in texture and taste to this popular bread. This is it! Makes 4 loaves.*

6 cups water
2 Tbsp. yeast
2 tsp. sugar
½ cup powdered milk
½ cup canola oil
1 Tbsp. salt
1½ cups honey
5 cups whole wheat flour
7 cups white flour

1. **In mixing bowl,** add water, yeast, and sugar. Let yeast dissolve for approximately 5 minutes.

2. **Add** powdered milk, oil, salt, and honey. Mix well.

3. **Add** wheat flour and then white flour, alternating 1 cup at a time.

4. **Knead** for 10 minutes. Let rise in bowl for 1 hour.

5. **Flour** work surface. Divide dough and form into 4 loaves.

6. **Place** in greased bread pans. Let rise again for 30 minutes or until loaves are 1 inch above pans.

146

Shauna Evans

7. Bake at 350°F for 35 minutes.

8. Remove from pans after 5 minutes and put on a wire rack to cool.

Tip: *When working with whole wheat flour, it is important to remember that flour should be added last to get the correct consistency of dough. It is also important to remember that whole wheat flour absorbs moisture more than white flour. So when making whole wheat bread, you will likely need more flour to create a soft and elastic dough.*

147

Multigrain Bread

This is one tasty and resourceful homemade bread. It utilizes leftover breakfast cereal and food storage items like potato flakes. Makes 2 loaves.

3 cups hot water
3 cups whole wheat flour
½ cup cooked old-fashioned oats
1½ Tbsp. potato flakes
¼ cup molasses
⅛ cup honey or sugar
1 Tbsp. salt
1½ Tbsp. yeast
⅛ cup oat bran
3 cups white flour
1 Tbsp. canola oil for coating bowl
butter for greasing loaves

1. **Combine** water, whole wheat flour, cooked oats, potato flakes, molasses, honey, and salt in large bowl.

2. **Stir** in yeast.

3. **Let** proof.

4. **Add** oat bran and white flour 1 cup at a time until dough ball forms.

Shauna Evans

5. **Knead** dough until smooth and elastic.

6. **Using** 1 tablespoon canola oil, grease a large bowl, rolling to coat.

7. **Place** dough in bowl and allow to rise until doubled.

8. **Punch** down and let rise again.

9. **Form** 2 bread loaves.

10. **Grease** tops of loaves with butter for better rising.

11. **Bake** in 350°F oven for 30–35 minutes.

✏ **Tip:** *When raising yeast breads, you want the room temperature to be around 80 degrees with no drafts. The perfect place to raise bread is in a turned off oven with the door closed. If the temperature in the room is too hot, it will kill the yeast. If the temperature is too cold, the bread will not rise. For a crispy crust, brush the top of the bread with butter when it is right out of the oven.*

Breads and **Rolls**

Desserts

Strawberry Fluff

Here is another dessert my mom would often make when I was growing up. I was always fond of any strawberry-cream combination. 12 servings.

½ cup butter, melted
1 (8-oz.) pkg. vanilla wafer cookies, crushed
½ (16-oz.) pkg. mini marshmallows
½ cup milk
1 pint whipping cream
1 Tbsp. powdered sugar
1 cup chopped walnut pieces
4 cups frozen strawberries, sweetened and drained

1. **Combine** butter and 2 cups cookie crumbs; press into bottom of 9 × 13 pan.

2. **In saucepan,** melt marshmallows in ½ cup milk. Cool.

3. **Whip** cream and sweeten with powdered sugar. Add to marshmallow mixture.

4. **In separate bowl,** combine walnuts and strawberries.

5. **Over crumbs in pan,** layer half of marshmallow mixture with half of strawberry mixture. Repeat.

6. **Top** with remaining cookie crumbs. Refrigerate for 1 hour to set before serving.

Shauna Evans

Almost Homemade Ice Cream

When you don't have time for homemade ice cream, this is a close second. It tastes almost homemade. 16 servings.

½ gallon premium vanilla ice cream, softened
1 cup frozen raspberries
3 firm bananas, sliced
1 (15-oz.) can crushed pineapple, drained

1. **In large bowl,** fold ice cream and fruit together.
2. **Place** in covered container and freeze until ready to serve.

Banana Boats

Since I was a teenager at girls camp, I have loved this dessert. After going to girls camp as an adult leader, I was determined to make this at home; a treat this good should be made at home too. 4 servings.

4 ripe bananas, peeled
1 cup chocolate chips
1 cup mini-marshmallows
4 (12-inch) squares tinfoil

1. **Slit** each banana lengthwise.

2. **Sprinkle** each banana with ¼ cup chocolate chips and ¼ cup mini marshmallows.

3. **Place** each banana on tin square. Fold up foil and roll top to seal packet. Place each banana on cookie sheet.

4. **Bake** in 350°F oven for 8 minutes.

5. **Remove** from oven and open tin packets. Return to oven.

6. **Turn** oven to broil at 400°F and broil for 2 minutes with oven lid open to toast marshmallows.

Shauna Evans

Bananas Foster

Elegant desserts like Bananas Foster are surprisingly easy. No need to enjoy this only at restaurants. It's a snap to make at home. 4 servings.

¼ cup butter
½ cup brown sugar
½ tsp. nonalcoholic rum flavoring
4 firm, partly green bananas, peeled and sliced
4 cups premium vanilla ice cream

1. **In hot skillet,** melt butter. Then add brown sugar and cook until bubbly.

2. **Add** rum flavoring and bananas. Cook for 4 minutes.

3. **Pour** ½ cup banana mixture over 1 cup vanilla ice cream. Serve immediately.

Apple Crisp

Apple Crisp is a wonderful fall dessert, when apples are freshly picked from the vine. Few dishes are dirtied with this method. This recipe brings out the best in crisp, sweet apples. Serve with sweetened whipped cream or vanilla ice cream. 12 servings.

6 tart apples
1½ cups old-fashioned rolled oats
¾ cup brown sugar
¼ cup flour
1 tsp. cinnamon
¼ tsp. nutmeg
¼ tsp. salt
½ cup butter, softened

1. **Peel,** core, and slice apples.

2. **Arrange** apples in a 9-inch square baking dish.

3. **In resealable bag,** mix oats, brown sugar, flour, cinnamon, nutmeg, and salt. Shake bag.

4. **Cut** butter into 1-inch pieces and add to bag and close.

5. **Knead** with hands to incorporate butter.

6. **Cover** apples with oat mixture.

7. **Bake** in 375°F oven for 40 minutes.

156

Shauna Evans

Hot Fudge Sauce

Even though you can buy quality hot fudge sauce, nothing beats homemade. Liquid chocolate is D-lish! Serve over ice cream.

1 cube butter
6 Tbsp. unsweetened cocoa
2 Tbsp. sugar
1 (13-oz.) can sweetened condensed milk
pinch of salt
1 tsp. vanilla extract

1. **Melt** butter in medium saucepan.

2. **Add** cocoa and sugar and stir. Heat through on low heat.

3. **Add** sweetened condensed milk and salt.

4. **Add** vanilla extract and stir to combine.

5. **Cook** on low heat for 3 minutes. Do not let boil.

Caramel Sauce

This sauce is for caramel lovers everywhere. Serve over ice cream.

½ cup butter
1¼ cups brown sugar
⅔ cup corn syrup
¾ cup evaporated milk

1. **In medium saucepan,** combine butter, brown sugar, and corn syrup.

2. **Cook** over low heat until mixture reaches soft-ball stage (235°F).

3. **Remove** from heat and stir in evaporated milk. Blend well.

4. **Store** in airtight container in refrigerator.

158

Shauna Evans

Pomegranate Frozen Yogurt

Sometimes it becomes necessary to find a way to make a certain food that you crave. Pomegranate frozen yogurt had this effect on me. I would go to Red Mango at least twice a week just to order this delicious treat. It got to the point that I had to either create this at home or break the bank. You will need an ice cream maker for this recipe. Serve with your favorite toppings. 8 servings.

4 cups vanilla Greek yogurt
⅔ cup sugar
⅓ cup pomegranate juice

1. **In bowl,** combine all ingredients. Stir to dissolve sugar.

2. **Pour** into canister of ice cream maker. Fit dasher. Follow directions on machine for freezing.

Homemade Lime Ice Cream

🍃 *As far as homemade ice cream goes, lemon and lime are my favorite, with honey being a close second. Lime ice cream is a flavor you can't buy in a supermarket, but it is incredibly creamy and refreshing. I made this recipe for a group of young single adults. They all came back for seconds and then thirds. You will need an ice cream maker for this recipe. 24 servings.*

2 qts. half-and-half
3 cups sugar
3 Tbsp. lime zest
1 cup fresh lime juice

1. **Mix** all ingredients in large bowl.

2. **Pour** into ice cream maker's canister.

3. **Secure** dasher and lid.

4. **Follow** machine's directions for freezing.

Shauna Evans

Buttercream Frosting

Everyone should be equipped with a buttercream frosting recipe. It is like the "gold standard" in home baking.

4 cups powdered sugar
¼ cup butter, softened
¼ cup half-and-half
1 tsp. real vanilla extract
pinch of salt
food coloring of choice

1. **Cream** sugar and butter.

2. **Add** half-and-half, vanilla, salt, and food coloring.

3. **If needed,** add more sugar or half-and-half, 1 tablespoon at a time, for correct consistency.

4. **Beat** until fluffy.

Desserts

English Toffee

From the time I was a young girl, my mom would pull out a special, heavy-duty, stainless steel pan each Christmas to make English Toffee. She still gives this classic treat out to her neighbors. One woman even asked her to give her a tutorial on making it. 24 servings.

2 cubes butter
1 cup sugar
2 Tbsp. water
3 cups walnut pieces, crushed fine
1 giant (7-oz.) Hershey milk chocolate bar, broken into pieces

1. **In large,** heavy saucepan, cook butter, sugar, and water on high heat until mixture resembles the color of a brown paper bag.

2. **In baking pan,** spread 1½ cups walnuts evenly.

3. **Pour** toffee evenly over nuts.

4. **Sprinkle** chocolate pieces over hot toffee and spread with a knife as it melts to cover completely.

5. **Sprinkle** remaining walnuts evenly over melted chocolate.

6. **Let** sit at room temperature to cool and harden.

7. **Before serving,** break into large chunks using a butter knife.

Tip: Have a brown paper bag handy to compare the color of the toffee to the bag. This is easier than using a candy thermometer and is quite accurate.

Shauna Evans

Evans Family Award-Winning Fudge

❧ *This recipe won the Utah Valley Magazine 2011 Christmas Dessert Contest and was featured in the 2011 holiday issue. We have been making this fudge each Christmas for over three decades. We had never made the recipe public until November 2011. In 2010, my neighbor made forty batches to give to the nurses and doctors at the Utah Valley Regional Medical Center's emergency department. They all begged for the "secret" recipe. I am always delighted with the feedback I receive when I share this amazing fudge with friends and neighbors. 24 servings.*

2 (7-oz.) milk chocolate bars
2 (7-oz.) Symphony milk chocolate bars
2 cubes butter
1 cup walnuts, crushed
1 (15-oz.) can evaporated milk
4 cups sugar
2½ cups mini marshmallows

1. **In very large bowl,** break up chocolate bars. Add butter and walnuts and set aside.

2. **In large** saucepan, cook milk, sugar, and marshmallows on medium-high heat.

3. **Once** mixture comes to a boil, stir constantly for 7 minutes. Mixture will be bubbling rigorously.

164

Shauna Evans

4. **After** 7 minutes, immediately pour marshmallow mixture over chocolate bars and butter to melt. Stir with large wooden spoon until butter and chocolate are melted and no longer shiny.

5. **Pour** into a 9 × 13 buttered, glass baking dish. Let sit at room temperature for 20 minutes.

6. **Cover** and refrigerate for at least 8 hours to set—preferably overnight. Keep covered and refrigerated until ready to serve.

Tip: *Be sure to keep water away from chocolate or it will "seize," or harden. This fudge recipe is so smooth, it needs to be stored in the refrigerator, covered, or it will be too soft. Too often fudge recipes taste like frosting. This one is a true chocolate confection!*

Fresh Strawberry Pie

Fresh Strawberry Pie should never be made with a store-bought glaze containing over fifty ingredients. I feel strongly about that. Simplicity and few ingredients are best when preparing fresh fruit pies. Makes 1 pie.

1¼ qts. fresh strawberries
1 Tbsp. cornstarch
½ cup sugar
½ cup boiling water
½ (3-oz.) pkg. strawberry-flavored gelatin powder
1 baked pie shell
sweetened whipped cream

1. **Wash** strawberries and pat dry. Cut stems off tops.

2. **In medium saucepan,** combine cornstarch and sugar.

3. **Add** boiling water. Cook until thickens, about 4 minutes.

4. **Add** gelatin and stir until smooth. Remove from heat and cool to room temperature.

5. **Place** strawberries pointed side up in baked pie shell. Pour cooled gelatin mixture over strawberries.

6. **Refrigerate** until set, for 1–2 hours. Serve with sweetened whipped cream.

German Plum Streusel

Fortunately, I have a great number of recipes I adore, but this one is truly special, because it was my late grandmother's creation. It's simply scrumptious and gorgeous, and it reminds me of her. My grandmother was one of a kind, generous, funny, talented, and a good story-teller with a German accent. 24 servings.

1½ sticks butter (¾ cup)
¾ cup sugar (plus more for sprinkling)
2 eggs
¼ cup milk
4½ cups flour
2 tsp. baking powder
20–25 red plums

Streusel Topping

2 sticks butter, softened
1 cup sugar
2½ cups flour
2 tsp. vanilla extract

1. **In large bowl,** cream butter and sugar.

2. **Add** eggs and milk. Cream well.

Shauna Evans

3. Sift flour and baking powder.

4. Combine butter and flour mixtures.

5. Pack into cake roll pan with ¼-inch sides.

6. Wash and pit plumbs. Cut into fourths and place evenly over dough, skin sides down.

7. Sprinkle generous amounts of sugar over plums (this brings out the juice in the plums during baking).

8. Make topping: In medium bowl, combine butter, sugar, flour, and vanilla (mixture will be crumbly). Sprinkle topping evenly over plums.

9. Bake in 325°F oven for 40–50 minutes.

169

Chocolate Mousse Balls

❧ Chocolate Mousse Balls are a family favorite. My nephew would always request these for family gatherings—no matter the holiday. 16 servings.

3 (7-oz.) giant milk chocolate bars, broken into pieces
1 (12-oz.) container frozen whipped topping
1 pkg. vanilla wafer cookies, crushed

1. **Melt** chocolate in a microwave-safe bowl in 30-second increments.

2. **Fold** whipped topping into melted chocolate.

3. **Place** cookie crumbs in shallow bowl.

4. **Form** balls from chocolate mixture using an ice cream scoop and drop into crumbs. Roll to coat all sides.

5. **Place** chocolate balls in airtight container and set in freezer for at least 2–3 hours before serving. Store in freezer.

Shauna Evans

Macaroon Dessert

This is a lovely, tropical-tasting dessert.

1 pint whipping cream
1 Tbsp. powdered sugar
1 tsp. vanilla extract
12 soft coconut macaroon cookies, crumbled into small chunks
1 cup walnuts, crushed
½ gallon orange sherbet, slightly softened

1. **In large bowl,** beat cream, sugar, and vanilla until whipped.

2. **Fold** in cookies and walnuts.

3. **In 9 × 13 baking dish,** spread half of cream mixture, covering bottom of dish evenly.

4. **Spread** the softened orange sherbet over the cream layer.

5. **Follow** the sherbet layer with the rest of the cream mixture, spreading evenly over the sherbet.

6. **Freeze** until set, about 2 hours. Cut into squares to serve.

Sweet Cinnamon Biscuits

❧ If you need a tasty dessert quicker than scat, then this is the recipe for you. It is effortless to make, yet it tastes like you've slaved all day in the kitchen. 12 servings.

1 (11.25-oz.) pkg. refrigerator biscuits
1 cup whipping cream
1 cup brown sugar
½ cup pecans, crushed
1 tsp. cinnamon

1. **Line** biscuits in bottom of 9 × 7 baking dish.

2. **Pour** whipping cream evenly over biscuits.

3. **Sprinkle** brown sugar, pecans, and then cinnamon evenly over biscuits.

4. **Bake** at 350°F for 15–20 minutes or until biscuits are flaky and cooked through.

Shauna Evans

Gingersnaps

Gingersnaps are perfect holiday cookies. They are sugar and spice and everything nice. They are quick to make and chewy, and they contain the holiday seasonings that I love. 24 servings.

⅔ cup canola oil
⅓ cup molasses
½ cup brown sugar
1 cup sugar (divided use)
1 egg, beaten
2¼ cups flour
1 tsp. cinnamon
1 tsp. ground cloves
½ tsp. baking soda
¼ tsp. salt
¼ tsp. ground ginger

1. **In mixing bowl,** combine oil, molasses, brown sugar, ½ cup sugar, and egg.

2. **In separate bowl,** sift remaining dry ingredients, except for remaining sugar.

3. **Add** dry ingredients to wet ingredients. Mix well.

4. **Using** a tablespoon, make small balls from dough and roll in remaining sugar.

5. **Place** on greased cookie sheet. Flatten cookies slightly with bottom of a glass.

6. **Bake** at 350°F for 10–12 minutes.

Shauna Evans

Sticky Buns

Sweet and sticky is dessert fun. 12 servings.

2 pkgs. frozen, uncooked roll dough
½ cup butter, melted
½ cup sugar
1 Tbsp. cinnamon
1 (3-oz.) pkg. butterscotch dry pudding mix (not instant)

1. **In bundt pan,** arrange roll dough in a circular fashion.

2. **Pour** butter evenly over rolls.

3. **Mix** sugar and cinnamon together and pour evenly over rolls.

4. **Sprinkle** butterscotch pudding mix evenly over rolls.

5. **Allow rolls to rise,** covered with a cloth, for 6–7 hours at room temperature.

6. **Bake** at 350°F for 30 minutes or until tops are golden brown.

7. **Turn** rolls upside down and allow to fall on serving plate.

Award-Winning Chocolate Cake

This recipe has an interesting history. We kept this solely in the family for decades. It's a classic chocolate cake that people continually asked for—everyone wanted it on their birthday. Then my mother happened to put it in a ward cookbook. One of the owners of Magleby's Restaurant tasted my mom's cake and raved about it. A few months later, a strangely similar award-winning cake showed up on the Magleby's Restaurant menu. The mystery remains if it's our chocolate cake recipe, but we have a sneaking suspicion that it is. 12 servings.

3 cups flour
1½ cups sugar
1 cup instant sweetened chocolate milk mix
2 tsp. baking soda
1 cup canola oil
1 cup buttermilk
2 eggs
1 cup boiling water

1. **In large bowl,** combine dry ingredients.

2. **Add** oil, buttermilk, and eggs to dry ingredients and stir.

3. **Add** boiling water. Stir until batter is smooth.

4. **Pour** batter into greased 9 × 13 baking dish.

5. **Bake** at 325°F for 40 minutes or until toothpick comes out clean.

Shauna Evans

6. **Let** cake cool completely before frosting with Chocolate Buttercream Frosting (recipe follows).

7. **Cover** and refrigerate overnight for best flavor. (The frosting sets up like fudge.)

Chocolate Buttercream Frosting

6 cups powdered sugar
½ cup unsweetened cocoa
¼ tsp. salt
½ cup butter, softened
½ cup half-and-half
1 tsp. vanilla

1. **In medium bowl,** sift sugar, cocoa, and salt.

2. **Add** butter to sugar mixture and stir to combine.

3. **Add** half-and-half and vanilla to mixture. Beat until smooth and creamy.

4. **Frost** cake when completely cool.

Peach Cobbler

🍑 *Cobblers are not just for Dutch oven cooking. This cobbler is wonderfully good—peaches and cream at perfection. Serve with sweetened whipped cream or vanilla ice cream. 8 servings.*

3 lbs. ripe peaches
1 Tbsp. lemon juice
¼ cup brown sugar
1½ Tbsp. cornstarch
½ cup water
½ cup sugar (divided use)
½ cup flour
½ tsp. baking powder
¼ tsp. salt
2 Tbsp. butter, softened
1 large egg

1. **Peel** and slice peaches and place in 2-quart buttered baking dish.

2. **Stir** in lemon juice.

3. **In saucepan,** combine brown sugar and cornstarch. Add water, stirring until cornstarch is dissolved. Cook over medium heat, stirring constantly until sauce has thickened, about 5 minutes.

4. **Pour** sauce over peaches.

Shauna Evans

5. Prepare topping: Sift sugar (except 1 teaspoon), flour, baking powder, and salt together.

6. Stir in butter and egg until soft dough forms.

7. Drop spoonfuls of dough onto peach mixture. Sprinkle with 1 teaspoon granulated sugar.

8. Bake in 400°F oven for 40 minutes or until topping is golden brown and peach mixture is bubbling. Cool slightly on wire rack.

Sour Cream Sugar Cookies

Super soft sugar cookies were a quest of mine for almost a decade until my friend gave me this recipe. After I made it, I was done searching. The sour cream makes these sugar cookies incredibly soft and good. 24 servings.

1 cup butter, softened
1 cup white sugar
2 eggs
1 tsp. vanilla extract
3 cups flour
1 tsp. baking powder
½ tsp. baking soda
½ tsp. salt
½ cup sour cream
Buttercream Frosting (page 161)

1. **Cream** together butter, sugar, eggs, and vanilla.

2. **In separate bowl,** sift flour, baking powder, baking soda, and salt.

3. **Add** flour mixture to butter mixture. Stir to blend.

4. **Add** sour cream and mix.

5. **Refrigerate** dough for 1 hour.

180

Shauna Evans

6. Roll chilled dough out ¼ inch thick on floured surface.

7. Cut into shapes.

8. Place on cookie sheet and bake in 375°F oven for 9 minutes or until slightly golden brown on edges.

9. Frost with Buttercream Frosting.

Strawberry Yogurt Pie

In the 1980s, my mom made this every Sunday for dessert. And the funny thing is: I never tired of it. It's refreshing and not too sweet. 12 servings.

2 cups crushed graham crackers
¼ cup butter, melted
1½ cups whipping cream
1 Tbsp. powdered sugar
4 (8-oz.) pkgs. strawberry yogurt
1 (16-oz.) pkg. pre-sweetened frozen strawberries, slightly thawed

1. **Mix** crushed graham crackers and melted butter and press into 9 × 13 baking dish.

2. **In bowl,** combine cream and powdered sugar and then whip.

3. **Mix** yogurt and strawberries with whipped cream.

4. **Carefully** spoon yogurt mixture over crust.

5. **Cover** and freeze for at least 1 hour to set before serving.

Shauna Evans

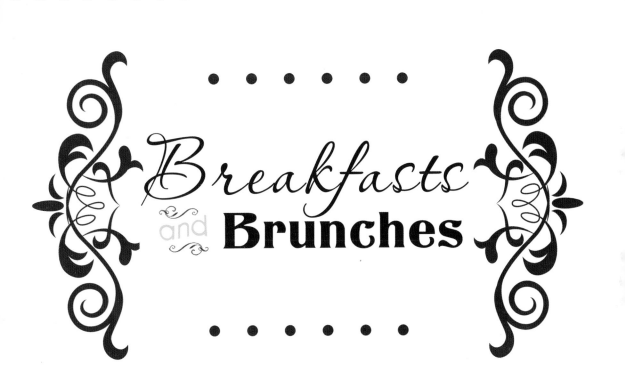

Breakfasts and Brunches

Buttermilk Syrup

Most of us don't go to the trouble of making homemade syrup, but this is so quick and easy that you may want to give it a try. Buttermilk Syrup is fabulous on pancakes, waffles, or French toast.

½ cup sugar
½ cup buttermilk
½ cup butter
1 Tbsp. light corn syrup
½ Tbsp. baking soda
1 tsp. vanilla

1. **In medium saucepan,** bring sugar, buttermilk, butter, and corn syrup to a boil.

2. **Add** baking soda and vanilla. Stir to combine.

Cider Syrup

This syrup is particularly delicious on Pumpkin Pancakes (page 193).

¾ cup apple cider
¾ cup brown sugar
½ cup corn syrup
2 Tbsp. butter
½ tsp. lemon juice
⅛ tsp. ground cinnamon
⅛ tsp. ground nutmeg

1. **Combine** all ingredients and bring to a boil.

2. **Simmer** for 20–25 minutes.

3. **Let** stand for 30 minutes before serving.

Shauna Evans

Crepes

🍃 *Even before I visited France, I loved crepes and made them often. But after going to Paris and ordering them from the street vendors, I'm head over heals in love with crepes. I have tried several recipes, and this one is the best! Top with powdered sugar and syrup, fresh fruit, hazelnut cocoa spread, or a squeeze of lemon. 12 servings.*

3 eggs
1½ cups milk
1 cup flour
1 Tbsp. butter, melted
½ tsp. salt

1. **In medium bowl,** blend all ingredients together.

2. **Using** ¼ cup batter, spread over hot griddle.

3. **Cook** crepe until slightly golden on one side.

🍃 **Tip:** *Savory crepes are just as delicious as sweet crepes. Anything you would put on a flat bread you could put on a crepe.*

Cinnamon and Raisin French Toast

Classic French toast is good, but Cinnamon and Raisin French Toast is even better. 4 servings.

3 eggs
½ cup half-and-half
1 tsp. sugar
½ tsp. vanilla extract
4 slices day-old cinnamon raisin bread
shortening for frying
Buttermilk Syrup (page 185)

1. **Beat** eggs, half-and-half, sugar, and vanilla together.

2. **Soak** each piece of bread in egg mix.

3. **In skillet** over medium heat, melt shortening.

4. **Cook** bread in hot grease until golden brown on each side, turning once.

5. **Serve** with syrup.

Shauna Evans

Morning Granola

⚜ This granola is not too sweet and is great as a snack, yogurt topping, or—my personal favorite—cereal. I get many requests for this recipe. 24 servings.

½ cup brown sugar
½ cup canola oil
½ cup honey
1 tsp. vanilla
4 cups old-fashioned rolled oats
½ cup walnuts, chopped
½ cup almonds, chopped
½ cup coconut flakes
¼ cup sesame seeds
¼ cup pumpkin seeds
¼ cup raw sunflower seeds
¼ cup oat bran
½ cup dried cranberries

1. **In large bowl,** combine brown sugar, oil, honey, and vanilla.

2. **Add** oats, walnuts, almonds, coconut, all seeds, and bran. Stir to coat.

3. **Pour** mixture onto large cookie sheet and bake in 300°F oven for 15 minutes.

4. **Let** cool for 5 minutes and add cranberries. Store in airtight container in refrigerator.

Shauna Evans

German Pancakes

This is the easiest, most impressive breakfast food. I made this for my husband when we were dating. His roommates were envious. Serve with generous amounts of powdered sugar. 12 servings.

> 12 eggs
> 2 cups milk
> 2 cups flour
> 1 tsp. salt
> ½ cup butter

1. **Beat** eggs until thick.

2. **Add** milk and beat again.

3. **Stir** in flour and salt.

4. **Melt** butter in 9 × 13 baking dish in 450°F oven.

5. **Pour** batter into hot dish with melted butter.

6. **Bake** for 20 minutes. The batter will puff, then fall.

Shauna Evans

Pumpkin Pancakes

Pumpkin Pancakes score high on my list of faves. They are unique and delicious. Try them with Cider Syrup (page 186). 12 servings.

2 cups flour
2 Tbsp. brown sugar
1 Tbsp. baking powder
1¼ tsp. pumpkin pie spice
1 tsp. salt
1¾ cups milk
½ cup canned pumpkin
1 egg
2 Tbsp. canola oil

1. **Combine** flour, brown sugar, baking powder, pie spice, and salt in bowl.

2. **In separate bowl,** combine milk, pumpkin, egg, and oil. Mix well.

3. **Add** flour mixture to pumpkin mixture. Stir just until moistened; batter will be lumpy.

4. **Cook** ¼ cup batter per pancake on hot, greased griddle until golden brown. Turn once.

Flapjacks

Everyone needs a really good flapjack recipe. This one is dang good; they are light and fluffy. I prefer flapjacks with real maple syrup. 12 servings.

1 tsp. salt
1½ cups flour
2 Tbsp. sugar
1 Tbsp. baking powder
2 eggs
1½ cups milk
1 tsp. vanilla

1. **Sift** dry ingredients in medium bowl.

2. **In separate bowl,** whisk eggs, milk, and vanilla.

3. **Combine** dry ingredients with wet ingredients.

4. **Cook** ¼ cup batter per pancake on hot, greased griddle until golden brown. Turn once.

Shauna Evans

Light Waffles

Waffles are so fabulous because they are great for breakfast, dessert, or even topped with savory ingredients. They look great and taste even better. 8 servings.

2 cups dry biscuit mix
1 egg
1⅓ cups club soda
½ cup butter

1. **Mix** all ingredients in bowl and then cook on preheated, greased waffle maker.

2. **Cook** until golden brown.

Egg and Bacon Soufflé

Oui! Soufflé. Très chic for breakfast. The Egg and Bacon Soufflé is savory and wonderful when paired with orange rolls and fresh fruit. 8 servings.

8 eggs
1½ cups half-and-half
4 oz. cream cheese, softened
1 Tbsp. cornstarch
pinch of salt
pinch of sugar
3 cups Monterey Jack cheese
½ cup celery, finely chopped
3 green onions, chopped
6 pieces of bacon, cooked until crisp and then crumbled
2 cups water
fresh salsa

1. **Whisk** together eggs, half-and-half, cream cheese, cornstarch, salt, and sugar.

2. **Stir** in cheese, celery, and green onions.

3. **Evenly line** 8 (6-oz.) ramekins with divided bacon pieces.

4. **Carefully** pour egg mixture into each greased ramekin, two-thirds full.

Shauna Evans

5. **Place** filled ramekins in 9 × 13 baking dish with 2 cups water in bottom.

6. **Bake** in 300°F oven for 25 minutes or until set and knife comes out clean.

7. **Serve** with fresh salsa.

Index

Index

A

Almost Homemade Ice Cream 153
Apple Crisp 156
Artichoke Dip 4
Asian Chicken 76
Asian Chicken Salad 24
Asian Dressing 25
Award-Winning Chocolate Cake 176

B

Banana Boats 154
Banana Bread 135
Bananas Foster 155
Beef Soft Tacos 80
Bleu Cheese Dressing 26
Bleu Cheese Lettuce Wedge 26
Broccoli Salad 28
Bruschetta 5
Buttercream Frosting 161
Butterflake Rolls 140
Buttermilk Syrup 185

C

California Citrus Dressing 33
California Salad 32

Cancun Grilled Corn 51
Caramel Sauce 158
Carrot Muffins 137
Cashew and Chicken Salad Croissants 78
Catalina Taco Salad 84
Cauliflower Soup 30
Charlotte's Zucchini Bread 144
Chicken Flautas 88
Chili Quick 82
Chocolate Buttercream Frosting 177
Chocolate Mousse Balls 170
Christmas Cheese Ball 6
Christmas Cranberry Salad 52
Cider Syrup 186
Cinnamon and Raisin French Toast 188
Citrus Tarragon Salmon 87
Clam Sauce over Angel-Hair Pasta 90
Confetti Squares 7
Cranberry Savory Chicken 86
Creamed Corn 54
Cream of Zucchini Soup 29
Creamy German Slaw 57
Creamy Herb Chicken Tetrazzini 94
Crepes 187

D

Delilah's Tacos 96

E

Egg and Bacon Soufflé 196
English Toffee 162
Evans Family Award-Winning Fudge 164

F

Fettuccine Alfredo 93
Flapjacks 194
Flour Tortillas 142
French Herb Cheese and Ham Spirals 12
Fresh Strawberry Pie 167
Fried Chicken 100
Fruit and Cookie Camp Salad 36

G

General Watts's Favorite Barbecue
    Spareribs 92
German Pancakes 192
German Plum Streusel 168
German Summer Salad 55
Giant Caesar Sandwich 79
Gingersnaps 174
Grandma's Dill Dip 8
Grandma's German Potato Salad 58

H

Homemade Lime Ice Cream 160
Honey Wheat Bread 146
Hot Chicken Salad 99
Hot Fudge Sauce 157
Hummus 11

I

Indian Chicken 83
Irish Potato Pancakes 62

L

Lemon Icing 145
Light Waffles 195

M

Macaroon Dessert 171
Mama Mia Pizza 108
Mama's Spaghetti with Red Meat Sauce 110
Mandarin Salad Dressing 45
Manti Barbecue Chicken Kebabs 112
Marinated Chicken Kebabs 114
Mexican Kitchen Carnitas 104
Mini Barbecue Meat Loaves 106
Morning Granola 190
Multigrain Bread 148

O

Old-Fashioned Lemonade 9
Orchard Applesauce 59

P

Pan-Seared Brussels Sprouts with Aioli
    Sauce 64
Peach Cobbler 178
Peach Muffins 138

Pink Sauce 67
Pizza Dough 143
Pomegranate Frozen Yogurt 159
Pork Barbacoa 102
Pumpkin Cheese Ball 14
Pumpkin Fruit Dip 15
Pumpkin Pancakes 193

R

Roasted Potato Wedges and
      Dipping Sauce 66

S

Salsa Fresca 16
Sloppy Joes 120
Sour Cream Sugar Cookies 180
Southwest Tortilla Soup 40
Spaghetti with Artichoke Hearts and
      Tomatoes 122
Spanish Rice 60
Spring Poppy Seed Dressing 44
Spring Rolls 70
Spring Spinach Salad 42
Sticky Buns 175
Strawberry Fluff 152
Strawberry Yogurt Pie 182
Stuffed Mushrooms 17
Sugar and Spice Steaks 117
Sunday Dinner Rolls 139
Sunday Pot Roast 124
Sweet and Sour Chicken 118
Sweet Baby Carrots 61
Sweet Cinnamon Biscuits 172
Sweet Potato Casserole 72
Sweet Potato Muffins 136

T

Tarragon Herb Butter with Salmon Steaks
      126
Toasted Garlic Broccoli 69
Tomatillo Ranch Dressing 37
Tortellini Soup 34
Tortilla Soup 47
Touchdown Taco Soup 48
Tuscan Tomato and Corn Chowder 39

W

Wassail 18
Watermelon Lemonade 21
White Chicken Chili 130
White Sauce 67

Y

Yogurt Chicken 119
Yorkshire Beef 128
Yorkshire Puddings 127

About the Author

Shauna Evans has been creating in the kitchen since age five, when she attempted to make a pie but actually made an incredibly adhesive glue. She has been cooking delicious dishes for family and friends ever since. Recently, Shauna has won over eight cooking contests, including Utah's Own Ultimate Recipe Roundup, Dream Dinners' National Recipe contest, *Utah Valley Magazine*'s Christmas Dessert contest, Barbecue Lovers' and Date Night Doins' BBQ Recipe contest, and B98.7's Celebrity Chef Throwdown Recipe contest. She was also one of Aetna's Healthy Food Fight finalists.

Not only does groovy mom, Shauna Evans, cook up recipes for contests, but she also loves to teach others how to make delicious food in their own kitchens. Shauna has appeared on *Good Things Utah*, *Studio 5*, and *The Daily Dish*. She has participated at *Salt Lake Tribune*'s home expo, in addition to teaching cooking classes across the state of Utah. She also brings an international culinary experience to the table. She has traveled to Europe, Japan, and Mexico, savoring different flavors and dishes to incorporate in her cooking at home. Shauna is a mother of five chocolate-covered children and is married to her biggest fan, Joe Evans. For more sweet and savory recipes, go to www.agroovymom.com.